The Violent Foam

New and Selected Poems

by

Daisy Zamora

Translated by George Evans

A Lorna - con mucho cariño y un gran abrazo - Daisy y

CURBSTONE PRESS

Conway - Abril 2003

FIRST EDITION, 2002
Copyright © 2002 by Daisy Zamora
Translation copyright © 2002 by George Evans
All Rights Reserved

Printed in Canada on acid-free paper by Transcon Printing /
    Best Book Manufacturing
Cover design: Susan Shapiro

This book was published with the support of the
National Endowment for the Arts, Connecticut
Commission on the Arts, and donations from many
individuals. We are very grateful for this support.

Library of Congress Cataloging-in-Publication Data

Zamora, Daisy.
    [Violenta espuma. English & Spanish]
    The violent foam : new and selected poems / by Daisy
Zamora; translated by George Evans. — 1st ed.
        p. cm.
    ISBN: 1-880684-88-8
    I. Evans, George. II. Title.
    PQ7519.2.Z35 V513 2002
    861'.64—dc21
                                    2002004255

Published by
CURBSTONE PRESS   321 Jackson St.   Willimantic, CT 06226
info@curbstone.org • www.curbstone.org

ACKNOWLEDGMENTS

Early versions of some of these translations were published in the following: *Heat* (Australia), *Ploughshares*, and *Southwest Review.*

The original Spanish versions of some of these poems were published in the following books by Daisy Zamora: *La violenta espuma* (Managua: Ministry of Culture, 1981); *En limpio se escribe la vida* (Managua: Editorial Nueva Nicaragua, 1988); *A cada quién la vida* (Managua: Editorial Vanguardia, 1994).

The author and translator wish to thank their many friends for spiritual support and encouragement during the creation of this book. We must name and thank a few friends specifically for being directly involved in the completion of this work, but any we fail to name who belong here may be certain of our friendship and respect. Forgive us: memory can be fallible after so many years of work. Demetria Martínez & Martín Espada gave this book its first spark of life with the gift of their friendship and unconditional support, followed by the less intangible gift of the best Spanish-English dictionary we could hope to own—it was all uphill from there. Demetria has been with us down to the last line in this book, to the final period, and her spirit is everywhere herein—we would not have it otherwise. Wayne Karlin is in a class of his own: brother in arms, brother in fact, and constant inspiration. The following friends each know what they have done to help and encourage us, and each is somewhere in the poems: Claribel Alegría, Jimmy Santiago Baca, Claudia Bernardi, Kevin & Leslie Bowen, Jean Coronel, Gloria Emerson, Abbie Fields, Bobbie Lousie Hawkins, Larry Heinemann, María Denise Marenco, Kasi McMurray, Grace Paley & Bob Nichols, Margaret Randall, Jovanka Solórzano, Roberto Sosa, Sandy Taylor & Judy Doyle, Eliot Weinberger, and María José Zamora.

Last, but never least, our forever love to our printer's devils, Joaquín and René.

For George Evans

Es hielo abrasador, es fuego helado,
es herida que duele y no se siente,
es un soñado bien, un mal presente,
es un breve descanso muy cansado.

Es un descuido que nos da cuidado,
un cobarde con nombre de valiente,
un andar solitario entre la gente,
un amar solamente ol ser amado.

Es una libertad encarcelada,
que dura hasta el postrero paroxismo;
enfermedad que crece si es curada.

Este es el niño Amor, éste es su abismo,
¡Mirad cuánta amistad tendrá con nada
el que en todo es contrario de sí mismo!

Francisco de Quevedo y Villegas

CONTENTS

Death Abroad / *Muerte Extranjera*

Fairy Tales / *Cuentos de Hadas*

We Take You for Granted / *Contamos con que estás*

Urgent Message to My Mother / *Mensaje urgente a mi madre*

No-Man's-Land / *Tierra de nadie*

A Chunk of Violent Foam

Guárdame un trozo de violenta espuma ...
Keep for me a chunk of violent foam ...
Pablo Neruda

All writing takes the writer on a journey, but translation is an expedition, complete with flashes of culture shock, exotica, and that state of exhilarated exhaustion every serious traveler (and every serious writer) learns to savor as rare and gratifying. If on that expedition one is fortunate enough to have the exquisite, engaging company of the poet Daisy Zamora, the experience becomes pure adventure.

Though credited as translator of this work, I am so only to the degree that without the complete collaboration of the author, I would not even have attempted it. It's not that the original work is so difficult to understand, or even remotely abstract, but that its hard-won simplicity, beautiful music, and cultural references exist in the realm of the nearly untranslatable, a condition and mark of all genuine poetry. I can speak then only as co-translator, a sort of archeologist of poetry, a lucky traveler who met a kindred spirit and guide, pausing temporarily with this book, anxious to continue the forward motion it created.

In the years it took us to complete these translations, years in which an immense cultural and literary exchange took place for both of us, we worked to create a voice that would resonate with tones, rhythms, and forms as close to the original poems as possible. It was a daunting but rewarding effort, and it's up to Daisy's readers to judge the results. In addition to welcomed, stable periods of sustained work, especially near the end, we were at times forced to communicate difficult concepts and texts over vast distances, worked during the vigorous chaos of being on the road for poetry events, spent one long period surviving the rigors of a harsh and remote desert region (no small feat for a poet from tropical Nicaragua), and spent every available moment deciding the best way to express difficult words, phrases, or images, taking great care to keep the music and language, the double heart of poetry, intact.

The poems eventually found their own voice in English, and started coming to life in spite of us at times. Before embarking on this project, I thought satisfying, correct translations of poetry were impossible to hope for, mainly because of the stubborn way poetry insists on being true only to its native culture and language. I no longer believe that, and have come to an even deeper appreciation for earlier poetry translators I've always admired, most notably Cid Corman, Kenneth Rexroth, and Ezra Pound.

Daisy and I were transformed by this work, almost literally melting into one another, to the degree that her children became my children, her family became my family, mine became hers, and we had the extraordinary experience of blending artistic ideals we both held before we met. Poetry was the foundation and motivation for both our lives when we met—in fact, poetry was literally the reason we met—but unlike her, I had not witnessed poetry as an effective social or political force. Despite a fulfilling life in poetry, and positive experiences directing a massive national public poetry project, I believed then, and still do, that except for unusual brief moments, poetry is not destined for wide and sustained acknowledgment in the United States. Nevertheless, my love for the art has remained firmly intact, without bitterness, and my optimistic pessimism is unshaken (this last a term Daisy and I learned from our friend Honduran poet Roberto Sosa). That perspective, and an open mind, was useful when I met Daisy, because her experience with poetry as a cultural force and living entity was the opposite. She comes from a world where poetry not only matters but makes a difference.

In the United States, poetry has never enjoyed the historical relevance it has in Nicaragua, or in the rest of Latin America for that matter, and it never will, unless we're fortunate enough to see that aspect of Latin American influence become so strong we can't avoid it—that is, if Latin America doesn't become so "Americanized" its own poets get pushed to the margins. Such a thing seems unthinkable at first glance (and I would like it to be unthinkable forever), but McDonald's, Hollywood, and the WTO have ways of clear-cutting complex societies almost over night.

Still, in all likelihood, grim possibilities aside, Nicaraguan poets and writers will probably prevail. They live in a world and milieu (shared by other Latin American countries) where everyone seems interested in poetry, tries to write it, recites it, and where the people not only read their poets, but quote them, respect them, and send them out into the world as trusted ambassadors and representatives. The tradition of poetry is particularly strong in Nicaragua, and is so intertwined with the country's modern history that it's impossible to separate one from the other. I feel confident saying that in Daisy Zamora's country poetry leads to and from everything, and that in Daisy Zamora's life it is the same.

The culture of her beloved Nicaragua comes vividly to life in her poetry, and so does its language, *Nicaragüense*, a graceful, colorful Spanish sprinkled with phrases and sounds from indigenous *Náhuatl*, rooted in the ancient language of the Maya. That language is her natural form of expression, and she has been writing poems in it for as long as she can remember, a practice woven into her earliest memories of childhood, and she is, without doubt, a direct artistic descendent of the first great Nicaraguan poet, Rubén Darío.

Born in Managua, she's from a very old and active family that has been politically and culturally influential in many aspects of Nicaragua's development since its independence from Spain in the nineteenth century. The history of her family, with its many branches, is one of important intellectuals, artists, poets, writers, ambassadors, politicians (including a president of Nicaragua and a president of El Salvador), scientists, historians, doctors, and other notable figures in Nicaraguan history, all of which I point out to emphasize the depths and strength of her Nicaraguan roots. Her childhood, which she remembers with vivid clarity in her work, and in conversation, was spent in what she has described as a lost era, a dream-like, innocent time shattered by the ever darkening ambitions of a cruel and murderous dictator, Anastasio Somoza Debayle, and his family.

Raised in a household ever aware of the Somozas, the household of an extended family historically opposed and resistant to the many U.S. interventions Nicaragua has survived, her youth was a world filled with the voices of people coming and going with opinions, news and plans. She grew up paying close attention to the details of politics, political developments and intrigues. Educated in a Catholic school under the vigilant eyes of nuns, she became actively involved in politics at seventeen, soon after entering the university. Nicaraguan universities represented the greatest source of resistance to the ever-repressive Somoza regime, begun by Anastasio Somoza García in the 1930s, and it was only natural for her to be part of the movement that developed into what became the Sandinista Revolution, named in honor of Augusto César Sandino, nationalist hero assassinated by the first Somoza.

During that revolution (a popular uprising by Nicaraguans of all classes, one that as a struggle for independence shared many ideals comparable to those of our own American Revolution), she experienced a life of clandestine resistance, lived the life of a soldier in active combat, and ultimately became the voice of underground Radio Sandino while in political exile. In the last few days of the revolution, she returned to enjoy the moment of triumph her generation brought to Nicaragua, and became the Vice-Minister of Culture for the new government. It's important to keep in mind that before, during, and after the revolution she was always an active poet, so it was yet another natural development for her to be involved in the cultural life that flowered after so much death and destruction.

In her new public role, she worked closely with poet Ernesto Cardenal, the Minister of Culture, and her time was spent helping to develop a complete revival of Nicaraguan arts ranging from native cooking to handicrafts, from folk art to its incomparable literature, and contributing to what became a successful national literacy campaign. She also traveled the world as a cultural representative, drawing international attention and support to a country made fragile by war but even dearer than ever to its citizens, who were energized by their hard won liberation.

What happened next is a story for another time, and it's best that I leave it to the poet to tell when she is ready. Let me turn back to the work at hand.

In 1994, Nicaraguan novelist Sergio Ramírez wrote an informative introductory essay to her book *A cada quién la vida* (*From Each One Life*), a collection from which some of these poems were selected, and it's appropriate to quote that to help establish a context for the work in this book. The title of his essay is "No-man's Land, Everyone's Land," and although the translation is by another friend, Abbie Fields, I'm solely responsible for any lapses or errors. Ramírez wrote:

> I have always tried to explain to myself the phenomenon of Nicaraguan poetry as an organic process, very unique and distinct in its voices, diverse but articulate if appreciated as a whole. The matter is not to explain the mystery of it, but no other phenomenon marks, in such a constant way, the rising development of our national culture the way poetry does. It is like a voltaic arc, still open, rising from the pole of Rubén Darío and extending itself over time with a diversity of light and intensity of splendor.
>
> And as I say, it's not a matter of explaining the mystery, but neither do I want to explain why the flashing trail that voltaic arc extends in its incessant progress is charged, at the end of the century, with the voices of women. They are seductive voices, different from one another, incomparable, each possessing its own certainty, own sense and sensibility, own passion.
>
> Daisy Zamora has her own history and her own voice in this concert, and has produced an extensive body of work that permits us to make some general observations. As a reader of poetry, she has been among my favorites for years, and with each new book she has reaffirmed that preference.
>
> She sings about everyday life, which is the most difficult art form of all, and achieving excellence while lyrically painting domestic life, daily pain and happiness, requires walking a razor's edge. ...For those who write poetry, men or women, a certain sensibility common to both sexes is needed (if there isn't one, there is nothing), something referred to as a grace, a blessing, or unction. The numen, or spirit. After that comes the most arduous task, translating grace into words, translating feelings, perceptions, memories and imagination into language. And that language is an orchestration, with each word in its place, with harmony, rhythm, form, architecture, texture, and a framework. The word, so elusive and fickle.

...It is precisely here that Daisy Zamora always passes the test with flying colors, and with style. ...[Her] work gives life to poetry about daily existence, and converts any negative implications in the word "domestic" to positive ones. She makes it possible for torrents of life to spring forth from daily, domestic reality. Her sensual milieu is life itself, and she's able to translate and interpret the sensations and perceptions of that life into words.

Family tradition, childhood memory, disillusionment, suffering, grief, happiness and serenity, agony and death. These are the glories of daily life. ...But the domestic, and the home which is always the beacon, reach a transcendental level in her poetry, precisely because they do not resort to a mere outer recounting, a superficial chronicle, but are instead a rigorous and painful examination of feelings, where the key to sensibility is. The origin and the consequence. The mask of the dead, and the pain of the living.

Grandparents, mothers, uncles, and sisters all pass through a sieve that removes superfluous pomp from their lineage and bestows upon them an intimate depth. The family in the heart, and in the clenched, tightened fist. The memory of what has been lived, and the final seal of death, equally beautify souls, bodies, hands and faces. ...

Poets becomes transcendent when, in the act of choosing their own universe...they succeed in selecting an appropriate language for it. That is the word, the essential connection between sensibility and expression. These poems have a precise, colloquial, sensual, delicate and often epigrammatic texture, precisely because there is irony behind the pain. All of these elements are the true attributes of the word.

...From a chronicle of family memories, sepia-colored nostalgia, celebrating a woman's body as her own temple, exalting her daily pain, these pages overflow with a wise torrent, culminating in lyrical protest: freedom springs from rebellion. ...For the family, life. For the dead, life.

For woman, life. For the writer herself, life. This is a necessary chronicle...a celebration of life.

But as Sergio Ramírez would agree, because of the rich and extraordinary nature of her life experience, coupled with a relentless curiosity, the range of Daisy Zamora's poetry (which often does embrace the ostensibly dull, weary details of quotidian life) has as its outer limits a healthy interest in the universe at large, which is the true spirit of genuine poetry. In his book *Aesthetics and Revolution: Nicaraguan Poetry, 1979-1990*, the scholar Greg Dawes cautions us to be careful when drawing conclusions about the personal nature of her work. He points out that her 1988 collection *En limpio se escribe la vida* (*Life Written on a Clean Slate*) was, for Nicaragua, "the first poetic and feminist manifesto that undermines patriarchal definitions of the family, reproduction, housework, and the 'double day.'" But he reminds us that while "individual experience is certainly implicit in Zamora's work, it is not her overriding concern; rather, the actual incidents she describes are caught within a network of social signification...and the poet makes a conscious effort to keep these issues in the foreground and undermine their very logic." Which is to say, and note, there is a broader purpose to the most seemingly mundane aspects of her work, and to interpret her poems as simply confessional or personal would be mistaken.

She could not possibly be all of the people who speak through her poetry, but mixed in with the delicate, sometimes ephemeral beauty of her imagery and music, is a gritty realism and humor that mark her art in a way that convinces a reader it could only come from the source, only be spoken from the heart of one who went through it, one who was there, who survived. Hers is such a genuine voice we cannot separate the dance from the dancer, to paraphrase W.B. Yeats, and the borders of reality and sharp observation are blurred over and over throughout her work, from war poetry to love poetry, from first person monologue to impressionistic vignettes, from confessions to revelations, throughout the range of her passionate and compassionate body of poems.

This bilingual book includes new poems (some of which are published here for the first time in either language), and work selected from her three poetry books in Spanish. A fourth collection, including all of her new poems, will soon be published in Managua. It's reasonable to estimate that this new translation represents about a third of her overall work, and I make that point only to claim sympathy for how difficult it was to decide what to include in this selection. It's a tribute to this poet's appeal that her poetry has been translated into many languages over the years, and that there have been three other book-length English translations of her work (two in the US and one in England). The US volumes (*Clean Slate*, translated by Margaret and Elinor Randall, and *Riverbed of Memory*, translated by Barbara Paschke) contributed greatly to introducing her work to a wide audience in this country.

The invitation to publish a collection of new translations was welcomed by both of us, and having the author (who reads and speaks English fluently) involved in the translation and editing process from beginning to end, has resulted in work I can only describe as organic and as close to the original poems as possible, at least from our perspective. Our decision to retranslate some previously translated work was necessitated by the overall editorial concept of this collection—we wanted all the English versions to reflect the voices, tones and music that evolved from our work together—plus it gave the poet an opportunity to connect work from different periods, work she has long felt belongs together.

In many ways, Ambrose Bierce's dark observation is true: "War is god's way of teaching Americans geography." But there are better ways to learn about the world. In addition to reading history, one way (sometimes difficult but always rewarding) is the preferred way as far as I'm concerned, something Daisy Zamora not only agrees with but exemplifies: through the arts, which represent the best intentions of human endeavor, the complexity of life harnessed briefly into expressions of emotion, intellect, combinations of both, history, dreams, and all realities. In this case, with this book, the way to another world is through poetry, a truly ancient art. How lucky we are to come upon this particular poet, alive and in her prime, to show us how to get there.

George Evans, San Francisco, 2002

THE VIOLENT FOAM
New and Selected Poems

FROM EACH ONE LIFE

A CADA QUIÉN LA VIDA

A CADA QUIÉN LA VIDA

A cada quién la vida le extrae un rostro.

No hablo de pómulos,
de narices rectas, ni de cejas, ni de ojos,
ni de arrugas en la frente,
ni de mejillas y párpados
colgantes
          sino de aquello inocultable
o irreparable por cirugías o afeites.

Hablo de la miseria y el horror
de la mezquindad y el gozo,
de la crueldad o la conmiseración
que vislumbramos —no sabemos cuándo—
en el rostro del otro
que sorpresivamente es nuestro rostro.

FROM EACH ONE LIFE

From each one life draws a face.

I'm not talking about cheekbones,
perfect noses, eyebrows, eyes,
wrinkled foreheads
sagging cheeks or
eyelids
          but of what is impossible to hide
or fix with surgery or make-up.

I'm talking about the misery and horror
meanness and joy,
the cruelty or compassion
we see, without warning,
on someone else's face
surprisingly our own.

DAGUERROTIPO DE LA MADRE

Todo lo entendiste perfectamente:
la época, los límites, el lugar que ocupabas.

Tu inteligencia se desperdició en minucias.
Invertiste tu talento en administrar la despensa
y organizar el servicio de la casa.
Tu imaginación fue confinada a la vulgaridad
de lo doméstico.

¡Cómo resistías con los labios cerrados
y el llanto naufragaba antes de alcanzar tus ojos!

Pero tu dignidad nutrió mi rebeldía,
y tu silencio mi voluntad de hablar.

DAGUERREOTYPE OF A MOTHER

You understood everything perfectly:
the epoch, the limits, your place.

Your intelligence was wasted on petty details.
You invested your talent in managing the pantry,
organizing the household,
your imagination confined
to common housework.

How you put up with it, kept your mouth shut,
sank your tears before they surfaced!

But your dignity nourished my rebellion,
and your silence my will to speak out.

OTILIA PLANCHADORA

Al ritmo de la Sonora Matancera
Otilia pringa la ropa,
la dobla en grandes tinas de aluminio
            y panas enlozadas,
y no sé si baila o plancha
         al son cadencioso.

"Los aretes que le faltan a la luna..."
Otilia los llevó puestos al baile
         del Club de Obreros.

(Ella tenía novio de bigotito.)

Otilia, frutal y esquiva,
entallada por el vestido
bailó, bailó, hasta que se humedecieron
oscuros sus sobacos entalcados.

En la barraca del fondo
—bodega de tabaco, cuarto de planchar,
albergue del relente de las noches
que refresca las tardes de verano—
Otilia guarda su plancha.
Sueña que Bienvenido Granda
           y Celio González
cantan para ella "Novia mía"
mientras se pringa la cara con lágrimas.

OTILIA, IRONING WOMAN

Otilia sprinkles clothes
to the rhythm of *Sonora Matancera*,
rolls and puts them into big aluminum tubs
        and enameled washbowls,
and I don't know if she dances or irons
        to the rhythmical *son*.

"The earrings the moon is missing . . ."
Otilia was wearing them
        at the Workers' Club dance.

(She had a boyfriend with a little moustache.)

Otilia, luscious and aloof,
danced and danced in her tight dress
until her powdered armpits were
darkened.

In the back cottage
—tobacco warehouse, ironing room,
shelter of cool night air
that refreshes summer evenings—
Otilia puts her iron away.
She dreams that Bienvenido Granda
        and Celio González
sing "My Girlfriend" just for her
while she sprinkles her face with tears.

Sonora Matancera, legendary Cuban big band; *son* is the most influential form of Cuban music—originating in eastern Oriente Province, it became a sensation in the 1920s, and the basis of contemporary *salsa*; "The earrings the moon is missing..." is a line from a popular *bolero* performed by *Sonora Matancera*, sung by Vicentico Valdés. Bienvenido Granda and Celio González were also singers in *Sonora Matancera*—"My Girlfriend" ("Novia mía") was one of their love songs.

ELEGÍA MÍNIMA

Acaba de morir una mujer sencilla.
Su vida de auxiliar de enfermería
fue útil a la especie.

No tuvo supermercados,
ni bancos,
no explotó a nadie.

Es decir, no fue dañina
como los magnates,
los dictadores,
los genios de las finanzas
y los politiqueros.

La noticia de su muerte
no será publicada
en ningún diario.
No hay campos pagados
presentando condolencias
a su familia.

ÁNGELA RAYO,
que esta frágil lápida
fije tu nombre
y guarde tu memoria.

MINIMAL ELEGY

A simple woman just died.
Her life as a nurse's aide
was useful to humanity.

She didn't own supermarkets,
or banks,
exploited no one.

That is to say, she wasn't harmful
like tycoons,
dictators,
geniuses of finance,
and those politicians.

The news of her death
will not be published
in any newspaper.
There will be no paid announcements
offering condolences
to her family.

ÁNGELA RAYO,
may this fragile gravestone
mark your name
and guard your memory.

LA MESERA (1)

De mesa en mesa
recoge las botellas vacías de cerveza,
apila los platos en la bandeja plástica,
y sus gruesos dedos, como pinzas
levantan de una vez
cinco vasos de vidrio
que hacen "clic" al juntarse.

Como un cometa gordo recorre su órbita:
el trajín enciende su rostro,
agita sus brazos y los pequeños pechos,
bajo el vestido celeste con delantal
que le termina en lazo
sobre las ancas.

Va
      de mesa
              en mesa,
hasta que las pláticas se arralan,
se apagan los ruidos de la cocina
y los clientes se dispersan,
dejan de pasar los buses,
y la luna se ve alta
sobre los postes de luz.

Al cerrar,
ella coloca las sillas sobre las mesas
y se sienta al fondo de la comidería.
Con dificultad se saca los zapatos,

THE WAITRESS (1)

She goes from table to table
collecting empty beer bottles,
piles dishes on a plastic tray,
and snatches five glasses
at once
her thick, tong-like fingers
clicking them together.

Like a fat comet she covers her orbit:
the rushing inflames her face
and shakes her arms and small breasts
under a sky-blue dress with an apron
tied in a bow
above her backside.

She goes
       from table
              to table,
until the chatter dies down,
the kitchen noises fade,
customers disperse,
buses stop passing,
and the moon is high
above the streetlights.

At closing time,
she puts the chairs upside down on the tables
then sits at the back of the diner.
With difficulty, she pulls off her shoes

encarama los pies sobre el taburete
y voltea las bolsas de su delantal
     para contar
          una por una
          las monedas del día.

puts her feet on a stool
and turns out the pockets of her apron
   to count
        one by one
        the coins of her day.

FIEL AMA DE CASA

Todo terminó con la Luna de Miel:
Azahares, cartas de amor, llantos pueriles.

Ahora reptas a los pies de tu señor:
primera en su harén,
tomada o abandonada según capricho.
Madre de los hijos de su apellido,
oreando tu abandono
            junto al tendedero de pañales,
estrujando tu corazón
            hasta despercudirlo en la ropa blanca.
Acostumbrada al grito, a la humillación
de la mano servil ante la dádiva,
mujer arrinconada,
            sombra quejumbrosa
con jaquecas, várices, diábetes.

Niña guardada en estuche
que casó con primer novio
y envejeció escuchando el lejano bullicio
                        de la vida
            desde su sitial de esposa.

FAITHFUL HOUSEWIFE

Everything ended with the honeymoon:
orange blossoms, love letters, the childish weeping.

Now you crawl at your master's feet:
number one in his harem,
taken or abandoned at whim.
Mother of children with his last name,
airing your abandonment
            near a clothesline of diapers,
wringing out your heart
            until it's spotless among white clothes.
Accustomed to shouting, and the humiliation
of a servile hand held out for offerings,
cornered woman,
            whining shadow
with migraines, varicose veins, diabetes.

Girl kept in a case
who married her first boyfriend
and grew old listening to the distant bustle
                        of life
            from her place of wifely honor.

LA MESERA (2)

Cómo creía entonces que de verdad
para algo me serviría el físico.
Morena y delgadita
sólo por mí venían los montones de clientes
desde Managua y Los Pueblos,
ya no se diga los que entraban
de aquí de Masaya.
Me tocaban las nalgas y tenía
ofertas al escoger:
De amorcito para arriba me trataban.

Claro que me acuerdo de vos, Castillito;
desde que te fuiste a México a estudiar
siempre pedí a los amigos
razón tuya.

Ya ves, cómo me tienen los muchachos:
gorda, cansada y varicosa.
Ni estoy tan vieja
pero así son las cosas de la vida;

La mesera más linda del "Mini-16 Rojo"
y de qué me sirvió.

THE WAITRESS (2)

How could I ever believe
my looks would do me any good.
Dark and slender,
tons of customers from Managua and Los Pueblos
came here just for me,
not to mention all those
from right here in Masaya.
They patted my ass and I had
many offers to choose from:
"Honey" was the least they called me.

But of course I remember you, Castillito;
when you went to study in Mexico
I always asked your friends
how you were.

See what having kids does:
fat, tired, varicose veins.
I'm not even that old,
but that's life, eh?

Most beautiful waitress of the "Mini-Red 16" saloon,
and look what good it did me.

LA MASAJISTA

Ella envidia a sus clientas:
hermosas y esbeltas
o irremediablemente gordas y decadentes
—la flaccidez preludiando el inminente derrumbe/
la herrumbre de la vejez—
pero las imagina amadas y satisfechas,
halagadas por hombres que gozan
de esos cuerpos tan cuidados,
mientras ella suda amasándolas,
estirándoles las carnes
palmeando glúteos, empujando
con sus nudillos muslos y caderas,
sobando espaldas, acariciando manos y pies
con furia contenida.

THE MASSEUSE

She envies her clients:
beautiful and slender
or inevitably fat and on the decline
—flabby prelude to imminent collapse/
the rust of old age—
but she imagines them loved and satisfied,
flattered by men who enjoy
those pampered bodies
she sweats while kneading,
smoothing out their flesh,
patting their butts, pushing
thighs and hips with her knuckles,
massaging backs, caressing hands and feet
with bottled up rage.

LA MESERA (3)

Con delantal y uniforme
como las otras,
pasa todo el día atendiendo órdenes:
"dos cervezas, un coctel de camarones;
la malteada de chocolate,
    un banana split,
        un arcoiris."

De un extremo a otro de la barra
sirve agua, pica hielo,
prepara dos vasos de té al mismo tiempo.
Abre el congelador, saca el helado,
mezcla leche, destapa cervezas;
arregla el coctel, tira las tapas al suelo,
coloca todo sobre la barra y sirve.

Parece igual a las otras,
pero es distinta:
        resplandece
cuando el novio atisba
tras la puerta de vidrio
    de la cafetería.

THE WAITRESS (3)

With apron and uniform
just like the others,
she spends all day taking orders:
"Two beers, and a shrimp cocktail;
a chocolate milkshake,
      banana split,
              and rainbow ice cream."

From one end of the counter to the other
she serves water, crushes ice,
makes two glasses of tea at once.
Opens the freezer, takes out the ice cream,
mixes the milk in, opens the beers;
arranges the cocktail, tosses bottlecaps on the floor,
sets it all on the counter, then serves.

She looks just like the others,
but she's different:
              she shines
when her boyfriend peeps
through the café's
      glass door.

ESTAMPA FAMILIAR

No hay esposo sentado en su sillón favorito
leyendo el diario con expresión beatífica.

Ni tiene pipa y pantuflas, mucho menos
bata de seda para estar cómodo en casa.

La mujer no es bella. Ni borda, ni teje,
ni sonríe al mirar a la hija
y al pequeño que juega.

No hay alfombras, ni mesa, ni florero,
ni lámpara de pie,
ni cuadros, ni cortinajes, ni hermosos ventanales.

Si hay perro, no es el que debiera ser.
(Tal vez un gato escuálido.)

La mujer está sola. El marido se fue
y no se sabe de él. La hija vende su cuerpo
para que puedan comer. En en suelo,
sobre un trozo de cartón duerme el pequeño.

Y ella tose, tose, tose, tose . . . insomne
toda la noche tose,
esperando a la hija
que vuelve al amanecer.

FAMILY PORTRAIT

There's no husband seated in a favorite armchair
reading the paper with a beatific expression.

No pipe or slippers, let alone
a silk robe for lounging at home.

The woman is not beautiful. She doesn't embroider, or knit,
and doesn't smile at the sight of her daughter
and the little one.

No rugs, no table, no flower vase,
no floor lamp,
paintings, drapes, or big beautiful windows.

If there's a dog, it's not the kind it should be.
(Maybe there's a scrawny cat.)

The woman is alone. The husband left
and there's no news of him. The daughter sells her body
so they can eat. The little one sleeps
on a piece of cardboard on the floor.

And she coughs, coughs, coughs, coughs . . . insomniac
who coughs all night,
waiting for the daughter
who returns at dawn.

FLASH-BACK PROFÉTICO

Todo en ella me recordó a su madre
a quien perdí de vista
desde que era muchacha:

Escarcha luminosa,
niña de cristal cortado,
ánfora translúcida.

Idéntica a su madre, que la acompaña.

—Y que ahora sonríe, se acerca y me saluda,
completamente en ruinas.

PROPHETIC FLASHBACK

Everything about her reminds me
of her mother I hadn't seen
since we were kids:

a luminous glow,
girl of cut glass,
translucent vase.

Identical to her mother, who is with her.

Who now smiles, comes up to me, says hello,
and is a total wreck.

LA COSTURERA

Toda mi vida sobre una SINGER 15-30,
y en las noches soñando con pespuntes,
jaretas, hilvanes,
mangas, vuelos, paletones.
Ni tiempo tuve para hombres,
siempre cansada y con dolor en la columna.

Yo, que era una chavala tan alegre,
la hija mayor, la preferida de mi padre.
Después que me arruinó tu papa
ya no tuve juventud,
sólo trabajo y más trabajo.

Te di vida, hijo,
pero yo no he tenido vida,
y ya ni sé cómo hubiera sido
de haber sido yo misma.

THE SEAMSTRESS

All my life bent over a SINGER 15-30,
and at night dreaming of backstitches,
tucks, basting,
sleeves, ruffles, pleats.
Didn't even have time for men,
always worn out and with back pain.

Once such a happy girl,
oldest daughter, favorite of my father.
After your dad ruined me
my youth was gone,
there was only work and more work.

I gave you life, son,
but I've had no life,
and don't even know how it might have been
to be myself.

NOTICIA EN EL SUPERMERCADO

... a vida é uma agitaçao feroz e sem finalidade
Manuel Bandeira

Entre las verduras oigo sus discusiones:
Hablan del supervisor, reniegan de los turnos,
de si la fulanita no llegó a tiempo
del mísero sueldo que para nada alcanza.

Hoy temprano hubo un accidente
en la carretera frente a mi casa.
Acababa de bajarse del bus una muchacha
y una camioneta la mató
cuando intentaba cruzarse al otro lado.
Un gentío rodeaba su cadáver
y algunos comentaban conmovidos
que no parecía tener más de dieciocho años.

De repente cesa la habladera.
Alguien dió la noticia
que se regó como un temblor oscuro y sordo
por el supermercado.

¿Cómo decirle a doña Mariana que su única hija
que tanto le costó,
que apenas iba a matricularse en la universidad
y se despidió tan contenta esta mañana,
yace en media carretera con el cráneo destrozado
mientra ella despacha muy amable la carne a los clientes?

NEWS IN THE SUPERMARKET

. . . life is a ferocious agitation without end
Manuel Bandeira

Among the vegetables, I hear their discussions:
they talk about the supervisor, grumble about shifts,
about so-and-so who was late,
and the miserable salary that doesn't pay enough.

> *Early this morning there was an accident*
> *on the highway in front my house.*
> *A girl stepped off a bus*
> *and was run over by a station wagon*
> *when she started to cross.*
> *A crowd surrounded her body*
> *and some were moved discussing*
> *how she couldn't be more than eighteen.*

Suddenly the talking stopped.
Someone brought news
that spilled like a muffled tremor
through the supermarket.

How to tell Mariana her only daughter,
raised in such hardship,
who was on her way to register at the university
and said good-bye so happily this morning,
is lying in the middle of the road with her skull crushed,
while she politely serves meat to the customers?

MARY ELIZABETH

Más de ochenta años esperó
Mary Elizabeth O'Brien
para ser libre, como lo fue
en un breve momento de su vida,
después de su niñez huérfana
y antes de casarse
con el que fue su marido
por más de cinco décadas.

(Le tuvo:
tres hijos, dos hijas
y unos gemelos
muertos al nacer.

Le soportó:
            gritos
            insultos
            groserías
            patadas
            y trompones.)

Cuando al fin enviudó, sus familiares
asombrados, no la reconocían.
Como pájaro que alista nido en primavera,
cambió alfombras y cortinas,
compró muebles,
pintó la casa y embelleció el jardín.

Porque ya nadie —sólo ella— recuerda
quién era Mary Elizabeth O'Brien,
la muchacha olvidada por todos,
que ha regresado, fugazmente,
un poco antes de su propia muerte.

MARY ELIZABETH

More than eighty years
Mary Elizabeth O'Brien
waited to be free, as she once was
for a brief moment of her life,
after her orphaned childhood
and before marrying
the one who would be her husband
for more than five decades.

(She gave him:
three boys, two girls
and stillborn
twins.

She withstood:
> shouts
> insults
> rudeness
> kicks
> and punches.)

When she finally became a widow,
her astonished family couldn't recognize her.
Like a bird preparing its nest in spring,
she changed rugs and curtains,
bought furniture,
painted the house and beautified the garden.

No one—only she—remembers
who Mary Elizabeth O'Brien was,
a girl forgotten by everyone,
who has returned, briefly,
for a while before her own death.

NERUDIANA OTOÑAL

Del brazo de su marido
que comparte
no sabe con cuántas más,
pero, en fin, su marido.

*Ella lo quiso, a veces
él también la quería.*

Procura recordarlo
como ella lo conoció,
antes de que se volviera
el que sería después.

*Ya no lo quiere, es cierto,
pero tal vez lo quiere.*

¡Si al menos por un instante
pudiera ser la que era
cuando él la enamoró!

*Es tan corto el amor,
y es tan largo el olvido.*

Pero frena el intento.
Sabe que si se atreviera,
todo lo perdería, todo.

Eso es todo. A lo lejos alguien canta. A lo lejos.

NERUDA READ BY AN OLDER WOMAN

Holding the arm of a husband
she shares
with she doesn't know how many others,
though, anyway, still her husband.

She loved him, sometimes
he loved her too.

She tries to remember him
as he was when they met,
before he turned
into what he became.

She no longer loves him, it's true,
but maybe she loves him.

If only for a moment
she could be who she was
when he fell in love with her!

Love is so short,
oblivion so long.

But she suppresses the impulse,
knowing if she dared
she'd lose everything,
everything.

That's all. Far away, someone sings. Far away.

DEATH ABROAD

MUERTE EXTRANJERA

LA EXTRANJERA

Intenta olvidar lo perdido
bajo algún cielo
que la nostalgia quisiera
confundir con el suyo.

Las risas de los hijos
—entrañables
donde todo es ajeno—
inunda de inocencia el aire.

Y toca la distancia
—pétrea y definitiva
como una lápida.

THE FOREIGNER

She wants to forget what's gone
beneath some sky
her nostalgia wishes
she'd confuse with her own.

Her children's laughter
—the one intimate thing
where everything is alien—
floods the air with innocence.

And she reaches to touch the distance
—stone-cold and definitive
    as a tombstone.

OLD BOOKBINDER'S RESTAURANT, FILADELFIA

A: Sandy Taylor

I.

Observo la animación
en el comedor atestado:
Todos conversan, ríen, ordenan
platos y postres exquisitos
mostrados como gardenias salvajes, heliotropos,
y orquídeas carnívoras en bandejas de plata.

Los meseros retiran los platos
con abundantes sobras,
postres apenas tocados por la cucharita
y apartados de la boca.
Eso es natural aquí.

En mi mesa solitaria,
bebo cerveza
y devoro ostras frescas de New Jersey
sin entender nada.

II.

Cuatro ancianas comparten una mesa
y brindan con voces apagadas
levantando sus copas temblorosas.

Después de la tercera ronda de *martinis*,
son cuatro muchachas bromistas y parlanchinas
que se yerguen airosas sobre sus propios cadáveres.

OLD BOOKBINDER'S RESTAURANT, PHILADELPHIA

For Sandy Taylor

I.

I watch the liveliness
in the packed dining room:
everyone is talking, laughing, ordering
exquisite meals and desserts
presented as if wild gardenias, heliotropes,
and carnivorous orchids on silver trays.

The waiters take away plates
piled with leftovers, desserts
barely touched by spoons
briefly tasted then cast aside.
That seems to be natural here.

I drink beer
at my solitary table,
devour fresh oysters from New Jersey
and don't get it.

II.

Four elderly women share a table
and toast each other with faded voices
lifting their trembling glasses.

After the third round of martinis
they are four joking, chattering girls
liberated from their corpses.

III.

En Filadelfia está Old Book Binder's.
En Old Book Binder's estoy yo,
una poeta de Nicaragua
    contemplando
        el despilfarro.

III.

In Philadelphia is Old Bookbinder's
and in Old Bookbinder's am I,
a poet of Nicaragua,
    contemplating
       the waste.

EL HIJO DEL CASERO
(Calle 19, La Misión, San Francisco)

La semejanza es innegable:

El porte,
los modos,
la piel descolorida.

Las mujeres siniestramente bellas
que lo acompañan,
los incisivos manchados,
y el aliento fétido
de sangre.

THE LANDLORD'S SON
(19th Street, The Mission, San Francisco)

The similarity is undeniable:

The demeanor,
the manner,
the colorless skin.

The women of sinister beauty
who accompany him,
the stained incisors,
and the fetid breath
of blood.

PROMENADE

Christina ofrece flores tan mustias como ella.

Jóvenes arrogantes, muchachas insolentes y bellas,
parejas que pasean con sus hijos, damas distinguidas,
hombres de negocios y ejecutivos mirando constantemente
sus relojes, pasan indiferentes.

Christina fue actriz, cantó en musicales de Hollywood,
actuó en Londres un tiempo, viajó por Inglaterra,
conoció a Ghandi, fue su discípula,
regresó a California . . .

Le has comprado el ajado crisantemo, que me diste.

Sólo nosotros, George, pudimos verla.
Ella es invisible. Un espectro que esculca
entre los basureros de Los Angeles.

PROMENADE

Christina offers flowers as faded as she.

Arrogant young men, insolent beautiful girls,
couples strolling with children, distinguished women,
businessmen and executives constantly checking
their watches, all pass her with indifference.

Christina was an actress, sang in Hollywood musicals,
was on stage in London, traveled through England,
met Ghandi, became his disciple,
then returned to California . . .

You gave me this withered chrysanthemum you bought from her.

Only we could see her, George.
She is invisible. A shadow digging
through Los Angeles trash.

LA JOYA MÁS PRECIADA

Este anillo que llevó
hasta la hora de su muerte
en sus dedos ancianos
con algún vislumbre de belleza:
zafiro circundado por diamantes,
era la ínfima vanidad de su pobreza:
las piedras son cristales
y el platino es imitación de platino.

Ahora es mi joya más preciada.

THE MOST PRECIOUS JEWEL

She wore this ring
until the moment of her death
on her elderly finger
with a vague glimmer of beauty:
sapphire encircled by diamonds,
a negligible vanity in her poverty:
the stones glass
and the platinum imitation of platinum.

Now my most precious jewel.

NOCHE DE JUNIO

Por la ventana del patio
entra el canto de los grillos.
Nada distinto me dice,
        nada nuevo.

Sonrientes fotos de álbum,
aparecemos lejanos.
¿De qué reíamos? ¿Qué hablábamos?
¿Qué muertes acechaban?

Por la ventana del patio
entra aburrido y eterno
—horriblemente eterno—
el sordo canto-chirrido.

JUNE NIGHT

Through the courtyard window
comes the crickets' song.
Nothing different it tells me,
                    nothing new.

Smiling photos in an album,
we appear far away.
What were we laughing at? What were we saying?
What deaths were lying in wait?

Through the courtyard window
comes the tedious, eternal
—horribly eternal—
tone deaf creaking.

CARTA A UNA HERMANA
QUE VIVE EN UN PAÍS LEJANO

. . . Y fui enviado al sur de la villa de Wei
—tapizada de bosquecillos de laureles—
y tú al norte de Roku-hoku,
hasta tener en común, solamente, pensamientos y recuerdos.

"Carta del desterrado," Li Po

Todavía recuerdo nuestros primeros juegos:
Las muñecas de papel y los desfiles.
Y a Teresa, la muñeca que nos caía mal:
Teresa-pone-la-mesa.

La vida no retrocede y deseo conocerte.
Re-conocerte.
Es decir, volver a conocerte.
Habrá, sin embargo, cosas tuyas que conserves.
Me interesa saber de tus lugares,
tus amigos, tan extraños a los míos
que hablan en otra lengua y buscan otros caminos.

Danbury, Hamden y Middletown,
Hartford y Meriden. Todos lugares
tan familiares a ti y a tus recuerdos.
A través de la sangre he vivido dos vidas,
múltiples vidas.

Los cocoteros ya están cosechando en el jardín
y el verano tiene rojas las gencianas del cerco.
Son hermosos y azules estos días,
transparentes y frescos.
Mis lugares amados son también los tuyos.

LETTER TO A SISTER
WHO LIVES IN A DISTANT COUNTRY

> *. . . And I was sent South of the village of Wei*
> *—carpeted by laurel groves—*
> *and you North of Roku-hoku,*
> *until all we had in common were thoughts and memories.*

"Exile's Letter," Li Po

I still remember our first games:
the paper dolls and the parades.
And Teresa, the doll we could not stand:
"*Teresa-pone-la-mesa.*"

Life doesn't go backwards and I want to know you.
To recognize you.
That is, to get to know you again.
Nevertheless, there must be things about yourself you still
preserve.
I'm interested in learning about the places you are,
your friends, so different from mine
who speak another language and search for other paths.

Danbury, Hamden and Middletown,
Hartford and Meriden. All places
so familiar to you and your memories.
Through our shared blood I've lived two lives,
multiple lives.

The coconuts are ripe for picking in the garden
and summer has turned the gentians at the fence deep red.
The days are blue and beautiful,
clear and fresh.
My beloved places are the same as yours.

Sobre miles de kilómetros mis palabras te tocan
como el pájaro que ahora veo posarse sobre un coco.

Prolongado ha sido el tiempo y la distancia.
Pero en uno de estos días luminosos
    (los rosales están repletos de capullos)
o de aquellos más lejanos del invierno
    (en todas las carreteras hay laureles florecidos,
    marañones y mangos y corteces amarillos)
con el último sol o en el primer aguaje
recogeremos los frutos
de la espera.

My words touch you across thousands of kilometers
like a bird I see right now perched on a coconut.

It's been a long time, and the distance great.
But one of these bright days
    (the rose bushes are full of buds)
or on some far away winter day
    (laurel trees are blooming along all the roads,
    and so are the cashews, the mangos, the yellow trumpet trees)
with the last sunshine or in the first downpour
we'll reap the fruits
of our waiting.

"*Teresa-pone-la-mesa*": Children's nonsense rhyme, mocking the doll.

LA INMIGRANTE

Se despierta extrañada
desconociendo el cuarto.

¿Adónde se fue el padre,
dónde la madre
que hace un momento apenas
la acompañaban?

¿Dónde están las palabras
de la conversación,
y el patio oloroso
después del aguacero?

Se levanta y suspira.

Este cuarto extranjero
y la luz indiferente
de una mañana cualquiera
que la hiere.

Desde la calle
los ruidos de la vida entran.
Y el sueño queda estrujado
como un pañuelo.

THE IMMIGRANT

She wakes up feeling odd
in a strange room.

Where is the father
and the mother
who just a moment ago
were with her?

Where are the words
of the conversation,
and the fragrant courtyard
after the downpour?

She gets up and sighs.

This foreign room
and indifferent light
of any morning
hurts her.

From the street
come the noises of life.
And the dream is left crumpled
like a handkerchief.

A UNA DAMA QUE LAMENTA
LA DUREZA DE MIS VERSOS

Sucede que cuando salgo, lo primero que veo
es un vagabundo que hurga en la basura.
A veces, una loca sombrea su miseria
frente a mi casa. Y el vacío de sus ojos insomnes
entenebrece la luz de la mañana.

Esquinas y semáforos invadidos por gentes
que venden cualquier cosa . . . enjambres de niños
se precipitan a limpiar automóviles
a cambio de un peso, un insulto, un golpe.
Adolescentes ofertan el único bien: sus cuerpos.
Mendigos, limosneros, drogadictos: la ciudad entera
es una mano famélica y suplicante.

Usted vive un mundo hermoso: frondosas arboledas,
canchas de tennis, piscinas donde retozan
bellos adolescentes. Por las tardes
niñeras uniformadas pasean en cochecitos
a rubios serafines.
Su marido es funcionario importante.
Usted y su familia vacacionan en Nueva York o París
y en este país están sólo de paso.

Lamenta mis visiones ásperas. Las quisiera suaves,
gratas como los pasteles y bombones que usted come.
Siento no complacerla. Aquí, comemos piedras.

TO A LADY WHO LAMENTS
THE HARSHNESS OF MY VERSES

It's just that when I go out, the first thing I see
is a drifter digging through the garbage.
Sometimes a mad woman is resting her misery in the shade
in front of my house. And the void of her insomniac eyes
casts a pall on the morning light.

Street corners and stoplights overwhelmed with people
selling everything . . . swarming children
throw themselves at the cars to wash them
for a peso, an insult, a punch.
Teenagers offer their only possession: their bodies.
Street people, beggars, drug addicts: the whole city
is a hungry, begging hand.

Yours is a beautiful world: luxuriant groves,
tennis courts, swimming pools where lovely
adolescents frolic. In late afternoon
uniformed nannies promenade blonde
angels in strollers.
Your husband is an important functionary.
Your family can vacation in New York or Paris
and in this country you're just passing through.

You lament my coarse visions. You prefer them gentle,
like the dainty cakes and bonbons you eat.
Sorry I can't please you. Here, we eat stones.

MUERTE EXTRANJERA

A: Francisco Zamora Gámez
y Rogelio Ramírez Mercado

¿Qué paisajes de luz, qué aguas, qué verdores,
qué cometa suelto volando a contrasol
en el ámbito azul de una mañana?

¿Qué furioso aguacero, qué remoto verano
deslumbrante de olas y salitre,
qué alamedas sombrías, qué íntimo frescor
de algún jardín, qué atardeceres?

¿Cuál luna entre tantas lunas,
cuál noche del amor definitivo
bajo el esplendor de las estrellas?

¿Qué voces, qué rumor de risas y de pasos,
qué rostros ya lejanos, qué calles familiares,
qué amanecer dichoso en la penumbra de un cuarto,
qué libros, qué canciones?

¿Qué nostalgia final,
qué última visión animó tus pupilas
cuando la muerte te bajó los párpados
en esa tierra extraña?

DEATH ABROAD

For Francisco Zamora Gámez
and Rogelio Ramírez Mercado

What lit landscapes, what waters, what lush greens,
what kite flying loose against the sun
in a blue morning journey?

What furious storm, what distant summer
dazzling with waves and salt air,
what dark tree-lined streets, what cool intimacy
of a garden, what evenings?

Which moon among moons,
which night of definitive love
under the splendor of stars?

What voices, what murmuring laughter and footsteps,
what faces grown distant, what familiar streets,
what blissful daybreak in a half-lit room,
what books, what songs?

What final nostalgia,
what last vision illuminated your sight
when death lowered your eyelids
in that strange land?

FAIRY TALES

CUENTOS DE HADAS

CUENTOS DE HADAS

Blancanieves se negó a ser sirvienta de los enanos,
y no le permitieron entrar a la casita.
La Cenicienta demandó por maltrato a su madrastra.
Sin escopeta no entro al bosque, dijo Caperucita,
después que el lobo la siguió por primera vez.
(Su abuela nunca abría la puerta sin asomarse antes.)

Piel de Asno se atrevió a denunciar el incesto de su padre.
La Sirenita no murió de amor. Tampoco se ilusionó
con que un príncipe se casaría con ella.
Cuando la Bella conoció a la Bestia, lo quiso tal cual era,
sin esperar milagros de ninguna clase.

Ricitos de Oro ni se atrevió a probar la sopa—
los osos la habrían devorado de inmediato.
La Princesa del Guisante no aceptó dormir
sobre tantos colchones, y les gritó que si dudaban
de su linaje, se fueran todos al infierno.

Alicia jamás viajó al País de las Maravillas
y la Bella Durmiente se acostó, aburrida,
porque nunca le permitieron hacer lo que quería.

Estos son los cuentos, hija mía.
La vida se encargará de contártelos.

FAIRY TALES

Snow White refused to be a servant for the dwarfs,
and was not allowed into their little house.
Cinderella sued her stepmother for abuse.
I won't go into the woods without a shotgun,
    said Little Red Riding Hood
after the wolf followed her the first time.
(And her grandmother never opened the door
    without first looking out.)

Donkey Skin dared to denounce her father's incest.
The Little Mermaid did not die of love, and had no illusions
that a prince would marry her.
When Beauty met the Beast, she loved him the way he was,
without expecting any kind of miracles.

Goldilocks didn't even dare taste the porridge—
the bears would have eaten her immediately.
The Pea Princess refused to sleep
on so many mattresses, and screamed that if they doubted
her lineage they could all go to hell.

Alice never traveled to Wonderland,
and Sleeping Beauty fell asleep bored
because she was never allowed to do what she wanted.

These are the tales, my daughter.
Life will make sure you know them.

REQUISITOS PARA SER REINA DE BELLEZA

Para aspirar a la corona
se necesita tener un cuerpo espléndido.
Además, lucirlo ante el jurado
sabiendo qué mostrar y qué ocultar
para que los hombres queden ávidos.

El maquillaje impecable.
Al máximo ojos y boca
que reflejen al mismo tiempo
sensualidad y candor / ingenuidad y lujuria.
Dientes blanquísimos son imprescindibles
así como abundante cabellera, corta o larga
pero cuidada y lustrosa.
(No puede olvidar que encarna un sueño.)

Alguna historia romántica que contar:
Novios que se oponen o esperan,
padres envanecidos que la alientan y admiran,
ilusiones de infancia que al fin se cumplen, etcétera.
Estudios y proyectos personales
con cierto aire intelectual, y sobre todo,
mostrar sensibilidad ante los males
que aquejan a la humanidad.
(Niños hambrientos y maltratados, injusticia social,
crisis económicas y guerras.)

La Regla de Oro es responder a todo
pero dando a entender que su cultura es mayor.

REQUISITES FOR A BEAUTY QUEEN

To aspire to the crown
it's necessary to have a splendid body.
Besides, you have to flaunt it before a jury
knowing what to show and what to hide
so the men are left eager.

The makeup must be impeccable.
Eyes and lips to the max,
simultaneously reflecting
sensuality and innocence / naiveté and lust.
Ultra-white teeth are essential
as well as abundant hair, short or long
but cared for and shiny.
(You cannot forget you embody a dream.)

You need some romantic story to tell:
boyfriends opposed to the contest or willing to wait,
proud parents who encourage and admire you,
childhood dreams fulfilled at last, etcetera.
Studies, personal projects
with a certain air of intellect, and above all,
a show of sensitivity to the evils
afflicting humanity.
(Starving and mistreated children, social injustice,
economic crises, wars and such.)

The Golden Rule is to respond to everything
implying you are more cultured than you seem.

Ya en el estrado, caminando de frente
se debe resaltar el pubis
y al darse vuelta
dejar al público borracho y enardecido.

Pero todos estos requisitos
serán insuficientes
si la dueña de ese cuerpo espléndido
no lo reparte espléndidamente.

Once on the platform, walking straight ahead
the pubis must be projected
and as you turn
leave the audience drunk and inflamed.

But all these requisites
will be insufficient
if the owner of that splendid body
doesn't distribute it splendidly.

LASSIE
(Autobiografía)

Es cierto. Fui fiel.
Mi único anhelo era que me pasaran
una mano displicente
por la cabeza.
Y moviendo alegremente la cola
daba vueltas, ladraba, me revolcaba
para recibir al amo.

LASSIE
(Autobiography)

It's true. I was faithful.
My one desire was to be patted
on the head
by a disdainful hand.
And happily wagging that tail
I ran in circles, barked, and rolled around
to welcome the master.

TEST PARA CONOCER AL MARIDO

—¿Olvida habitualmente felicitarte por tu cumpleaños?

—¿Te interrumpe cuando estás viendo tu novela favorita o leyendo una revista?

—¿Critica tu manera de conducir el auto?

—¿Considera que la casa no está bien atendida porque tú trabajas fuera y la descuidas?

—¿Si se enferma, te pide que estés pendiente de él constantemente?

—¿Siempre alaba a su madre y a su hermana frente a ti y a los demás?

—¿Cuando compras una falda, te dice con aire irónico que la falda está muy bien pero que te ves gorda?

—¿Lamenta estar casado porque si fuera soltero tendría mucho dinero para gastar en él mismo?

—¿Te reprocha pequeños gastos como esmalte de uñas o pagar un café a tus amigas?

—¿Se da cuenta si cambias de peinado o maquillaje?

—¿Elogia a las mujeres elegantes y diez veces más ricas que tú?

TEST TO KNOW YOUR HUSBAND

—Does he usually forget to congratulate you on your birthday?

—Does he interrupt you while you're watching your favorite soap opera or reading a magazine?

—Does he criticize the way you drive?

—Does he think the house is a mess because you have a job and neglect it?

—If he gets sick, does he expect you to be at his beck and call constantly?

—Does he always sing the praises of his mother and sister in front of other people?

—When you buy a skirt, does he tell you with an ironic look that the skirt is very nice but you look fat?

—Does he regret being married because if he was a bachelor he'd have lots of money to spend on himself?

—Does he reproach you for small expenses like nail polish or treating your friends to coffee?

—Does he notice if you change your hairstyle or make-up?

—Does he compliment stylish women who are ten times wealthier than you?

—¿Te dice con frecuencia: *cuando tú eras joven* . . .?

—¿Si estás enferma, te llama por teléfono
para saber cómo sigues o qué necesitas?

—¿Cuando salen al cine o a casa de amigos
te recuerda que lo ha hecho *sólo por complacerte*?

Piensa detenidamente las preguntas,
contabiliza respuestas y apunta el resultado.
No olvides que este es un juego intrascendente
sólo para distraerte un rato.

Seguramente sabes cómo es tu marido,
y lo has sabido siempre
sin necesidad de responder este test.

—Does he frequently say: *When you were young . . .?*

—If you're sick, does he call you on the phone
  to find out how you're doing or if you need anything?

—When the two of you go out to the movies or a friend's house
  does he remind you he has done so *only to please you?*

Think about these questions thoroughly,
count the answers and write down the results.
Don't forget this is just a trivial game
to entertain you a while.

Surely you already know your husband,
and have always known
without needing to take this test.

MARINA

Las muchachas,
bocas demasiado rojas,
ojos presos en círculos
demasiado negros.

Oscuras ellas como anguilas
contrastan violentamente
con sus trajes de baño.
Andan de week-end
con unos viejos funcionarios internacionales
que beben whisky
y pagan su compañía con ropas y baratijas.
Ellos generosamente las obsequian
con su más tierna halitosis
y sus impotentes taquicardias.

Cardúmen de sirenas o sardinas
lanzan las olas: guirnaldas y espuma.
Y brincan, brincando mejor en la playa ardiente
que en las camas otoñales.

SEASCAPE

The girls
with crimson lips
and eyes imprisoned by
black eyeliner.

Dark as eels
contrasting sharply
with their swimsuits.
Weekending
with some elderly international businessmen
who guzzle whisky
and pay for their company with clothes and trinkets.
They generously spoil them
with their tenderest halitosis
and impotent tachycardias.

A school of mermaids or sardines
tossed by the waves: wreaths and foam.
And they jump, jumping better on the hot sand
than in those old rotten beds.

CONSEJOS PARA ATRAER A SU ESPOSO

Cada parte del cuerpo requiere tratamientos
y cuidados especiales:

El pelo . . . cepíllelo mucho, lávelo a menudo
con abundante agua y acondicionadores.
Protéjalo del sol, escoja corte y peinados
que más le favorezcan. Y si usa tintes,
que sean los mejores.

El rostro . . . regálelo con cosméticos
de superior calidad. Límpielo profundamente
todos los días. Masajes delicados y descanso.
Cuando llegue el momento de rejuvenecerlo
no dude en recurrir a cirugía plástica.

Las manos . . . cuidadas son el reflejo
de alguien que tiene tiempo para tratarse bien.
Las pinturas de uñas deben ser
las mejores que vendan. Cada semana
arréglelas y retóquelas cuando haga falta.
Merecen lociones y cremas de igual calidad
que las del rostro. Manos finas
denotan a la mujer de clase.

Los pies . . . no se ven tanto como las manos
pero debe dedicarles igual atención.
Pula las asperezas con pómez o con paste,
busque zapatos cómodos y del cuero más suave.

La piel . . . debe tratarla con ternura:
es el frasco que envuelve el perfume exquisito

ADVICE FOR ATTRACTING YOUR HUSBAND

Each part of the body requires treatment
and special care:

The hair . . . brush it a lot, wash it often
with plenty of water and conditioners.
Protect it from the sun, choose haircuts and hairstyles
that flatter you most. And if you use haircolor
use only the best.

The face . . . pamper it with cosmetics
of the highest quality. Wash it thoroughly
every day. Delicate massages and rest.
When the moment to rejuvenate comes
don't hesitate to resort to plastic surgery.

The hands . . . cared for, these are the reflection
of someone with time to spoil herself.
Nail polishes have to be
the best on the market. Every week
fix and retouch them as needed.
They deserve lotions and cremes of a quality
equal to those for your face. Fine hands
denote a woman of class.

The feet . . . not as noticeable as the hands
but you must dedicate equal attention to them.
Buff the roughness with pumice or loofahs,
and search for comfortable shoes of the softest leather.

The skin . . . you have to treat it with care and tenderness:
it is the vase that holds the exquisite perfume

que es usted. Cuídela del sol, reconfórtela
con baños perfumados, aplíquele lociones
y cremas que la mantengan saludable y juvenil.
Y por supuesto,
haga ejercicios y tome abundante agua.

Si a pesar de haber seguido estos consejos
su esposo no le presta la menor atención,
desaparezca, bórrese,
rómpase como pompa de jabón.

you are. Protect it from the sun, comfort it
with perfumed baths, apply lotions
and cremes that keep it healthful and young.
And of course
exercise and drink plenty of water.

If in spite of following all this advice
your husband doesn't pay the slightest attention,
disappear, erase yourself,
burst like a soap bubble.

HOGAR, DULCE HOGAR

En esa hermosa casa de paredes inmaculadas
con un bello jardín de rosas y gencianas,
vive una muchacha.

La hermana mayor en cuanto pudo, se fue lejos.
Los hermanos maltratan a la madre.
La madre y el padre se destruyen mutuamente.

Pienso en todo esto, mientras ella
muy sonriente nos dice adiós
desde el portón.

HOME, SWEET HOME

In that beautiful house of immaculate walls
with a lovely garden of roses and gentians,
lives a girl.

As soon as she could, the oldest sister went far away.
The brothers mistreat the mother.
The mother and father are destroying each other.

I think about all that as she waves
good-bye to us with a big smile
from the gate.

CÓMO TE VE TU HOMBRE
(Pequeño Diccionario para Mujeres)

Si él se acuesta contigo
y estás a su exclusiva disposición
cada vez que te busca,
no clasificas para ser su *novia*.
Te presentará como su *amiga*.

Si todo lo crees, todo lo pasas, todo lo perdonas;
le prestas todos los servicios
y eres capaz de todos los sacrificios
sin esperar nada,
dirá que eres *buena*, que quiere decir *boba*.

Si es demasiado machista,
le entusiasma verte como *palo de hembra*.
Para interesarle
no hace falta que pienses,
sino todo lo contrario.

Si te cree *ingenua*, se acrecienta su ego:
el tímido se vuelve audaz,
el inseguro se llena de confianza.
Caperucita ideal para el Lobo Feroz
que se ríe de ti y te devora.

Eres *sexy*
cuando quiere decirte que le gustas, que le atraes,
que te ve sensual y te imagina erótica.
No te hagas ilusiones: esa visión dura
la primera etapa del enamoramiento
que es la de la ceguera.

HOW YOUR MAN SEES YOU
(A Pocket Dictionary for Women)

If he is sleeping with you
and you're at his exclusive beck and call
each time he requires,
you don't qualify as his *girlfriend*.
He introduces you as his *friend*.

If you believe everything, let everything go, forgive
everything,
serve him in every possible way
and are capable of all the sacrifices
without expecting anything,
he will say you are *good*, which really means you're a *fool*.

If he's really macho,
he gets excited seeing you as a *babe*.
To draw his attention
there's no need for you to think—
quite the contrary.

If he thinks of you as *naïve*, it increases his ego:
the shy one becomes daring,
the insecure one filled with confidence.
Ideal Little Red Riding Hood for the Big Bad Wolf
that laughs then devours you.

You are *sexy* means
he wants to tell you he likes you, he's attracted to you,
he considers you sensual and imagines you erotic.
Don't get your hopes up: that vision lasts
only during the first stage of infatuation
which is one of blindness.

Virgen es la imagen más apreciada por ellos,
pero todos están dispuestos a contribuir
a que dejes de serlo. Y si alguno lo logra,
contará que eres *tonta* igual a las demás.

Cuando él diga: *Esa mujer es una dama,*
es porque no encuentra otra cosa que decir.
Significa que te respeta y lo intimidas
porque no sabe cómo seducirte.

Aunque *mujer* parece un término neutral,
puede convertirse en despectivo
cuando él te dice: *Eso es asunto de mujeres.*
Pero si quieres ser *mujer inteligente*
aplaude sus ocurrencias, celebra su vanidad.
Pensar de otra manera es desastroso:
serás catalogada como *pedante* o *creída.*

Sensata es el concepto más trágico
que un hombre puede tener de una mujer.
Es aceptar el maltrato, las infidelidades,
ser sumisa y ahorrativa, comprensiva y nada celosa,
para que él disfrute de entera libertad.

Esposa significa cadenas y prisión.
Te ve como carcelera
de la que se esconde para enamorar a otras.
Eres la hipoteca sobre su vida
que firmó impulsivamente, y ahora le impones
la penosa obligación de los pagos mensuales.

Si ya no eres su *amor*, sino su *gorda* o su *vieja*
¡alármate! De estrella de la película
pasaste a extra,

Virgin is the image most appreciated by them,
but all are willing to contribute
to your not being one. And if one manages to succeed,
he'll say you're *stupid* just like all the rest.

When he says: *That woman is a lady*,
it's because he doesn't know what else to say.
It means he respects you but you intimidate him
because he doesn't know how to seduce you.

Although *woman* sounds like a neutral term,
it can become derogatory
when he tells you: *That's women's stuff*.
But if you want to be an *intelligent woman*,
applaud his witty remarks and flatter his vanity.
To do otherwise is disastrous:
you'll be classified *pompous* or *conceited*.

Sensible is the most tragic concept
a man can have of a woman.
It means accepting mistreatment, his cheating,
being submissive and thrifty, understanding and not at all jealous,
so he can enjoy absolute freedom.

Wife means chains and prison.
He sees you as a jailer
he hides from to make other women fall in love.
You're the mortgage owed on his life
that he signed on impulse, and now you impose
the terrible obligation of monthly payments.

If you are no longer his *sweetie pie*, but his *chubby-wubby* or *old lady*,
be alarmed! You have been demoted
from movie star to extra,

de joya reluciente, a pantufla vieja.
Y si te dice *inaguantable* o *pleitista*,
créele, porque te ve demasiado explosiva,
celosa, gastadora, posesiva,
y todos los "demasiados"
que se te ocurran.

Fea es como él te ve al cabo de los años
después de compararte con otras
más jóvenes y apetecibles.

Para que tu hombre te considere *única*
tienes que parecer una obra maestra:
bellísima, cariñosa, siempre de buen humor
y con tiempo para todo y para todos.
Cocinera genial, gran señora en los salones
y bomba sexual en la cama.
En resumen: Perfecta.
Perfectamente vacía y acartonada.

from shining jewel to old slipper.
And if he calls you *unbearable* or *bitchy*,
believe it, because he sees you as too explosive,
too jealous, a spendthrift, too possessive,
and whatever other "too"
you can think of.

Ugly is how he sees you after all these years
when he compares you with other women
much younger and more appealing.

In order to make your man consider you *unique*
you have to be a masterpiece:
wonderful, affectionate, always in a good mood
and with time for everything and everyone.
A brilliant cook, elegant lady of ballrooms,
and a bombshell in bed.
In short: Perfect.
Perfectly shallow and stuffed.

PARA DIRIGENTES Y DEMÁS HOMBRES

Los *buenos días* que das al llegar al trabajo
¿tu mujer los disfruta también?

La atención que prodigás a quienes te consultan
¿contrasta con el silencio que imponés a tus hijos e hijas?

El tiempo que invertís bebiendo con partidarios y amigos
¿es igual al que concedés a los tuyos en cumpleaños
y otras celebraciones familiares?

Cuando te preocupa dar explicaciones
¿te acordás de tus gritos si alguien en tu familia
se equivoca?

Cuando te señalan injustamente
¿pensás en tu costumbre de echarle a la mujer
la culpa en todo?

Si tenés que ser flexible en una discusión de trabajo
¿por qué en tu hogar nadie puede contradecirte
y deben aceptar que tu palabra es ley?

Cuando hablés en defensa de los pobres,
de los niños, de las mujeres,
de justicia, de voluntad de cambio y de consenso,
acordate de tu casa
donde toda tu furia, tu frustración,
tu impotencia por no tener un mundo a tu medida,

FOR LEADERS AND ALL OTHER MEN

Those *Good Mornings* you dispense when you get to work,
does your wife get one too?

The attention you lavish on those who ask your advice,
does it contrast with the silence you impose on your kids?

The time you spend drinking with supporters and friends,
does it equal the time you grant loved ones on their birthdays
and other family celebrations?

When you worry about explaining yourself,
do you remember how you scream when someone in your family
makes a mistake?

When you're unjustly singled out,
do you think about your habit of laying guilt for everything
on your woman?

If you have to be flexible in discussions at work,
why is it nobody at home can contradict you
and must accept your word as law?

When you speak out in defense of the poor,
of children, women,
of justice, of the will for change and consensus,
remember your home
where all your fury, your frustration,
and your impotence because you don't have a custom-made world,

la descargás sobre esos débiles
que aparecen en las estadísticas.

Acordate de tu casa
en donde no hay políticos
ni competidores
ni enemigos.

is dumped on the weak
who appear in the statistics.

Remember your home
where there are no politicians
or rivals
or enemies.

PRESCRIPCIÓN

Ni acupuntura,
ni té de hierbas,
ni antidepresivos,
ni inyecciones —señora—
la jaqueca se cura solamente
dejando a su marido.

PRESCRIPTION

Not acupuncture,
not herbal teas,
not antidepressives,
not injections—lady—
the only cure for a headache
is to leave your husband.

CUIDADOS INTENSIVOS

Totalmente desnuda yace entre las sábanas,
la misma que a los catorce años
fue estatuilla de marfil / bibelot de alabastro.
Su cuerpo marchito se mimetiza sobre la ajada blancura.
Su cuerpo —que nunca desplegó esplendoroso
en fotografías de centerfold
o belleza del mes en alguna revista.

Los hijos la contemplan
bajo la red de tubos, sueros y sondas.

Sobrevivió
al horror solapado,
a la crueldad del otro
dosificada en finos estiletes.

¡Quién la viera en el hermoso retrato
de aquel lejano día de sus bodas!

INTENSIVE CARE

Totally nude she lies among the sheets,
the same one who at fourteen
was an ivory statuette/alabaster bibelot.
Her withered body blends into the crumpled whiteness.
Her body—one never lavishly displayed
in centerfolds
or as beauty of the month in any magazine.

Her sons and daughters gaze at her
under the net of tubes, IVs and catheters.

She survived
the secret horror,
the cruelty of her husband
dosed with fine stilettos.

Oh, if only you could have seen her in the beautiful portrait
of their distant wedding day!

SER MUJER

A: *María Guadalupe Valle Moreno*

Haber nacido mujer significa:
poner tu cuerpo al servicio de otros,
dar tu tiempo a otros,
pensar sólo en función de otros.

Haber nacido mujer significa:
que tu cuerpo no te pertenece,
que tu tiempo no te pertenece,
que tus pensamientos no te pertenecen.

Nacer mujer es nacer al vacío.
Si no fuera porque tu cuerpo-albergue
asegura la continuidad de los hombres
bien pudieras no haber nacido.

Nacer mujer es venir a la nada.
A la vida deshabitada de ti misma
en la que todos los demás —no tu corazón—
deciden o disponen.

Nacer mujer es estar en el fondo
del pozo, del abismo, del foso
que rodea a la ciudad amurallada
habitada por Ellos, sólo por Ellos,
a los que tendrás que encantar, que engañar,
servir, venderte, halagarlos, humillarte,
rebelarte, nadar a contra corriente, pelear,
gritar, gritar, gritar
hasta partir las piedras,
atravesar las grietas,

TO BE A WOMAN

For María Guadalupe Valle Moreno

To be born a woman means:
putting your body at the service of others,
giving your time to others,
thinking only in terms of others.

To be born a woman means:
that you don't own your body,
you don't own your time,
don't own your thoughts.

Being born a woman means being born in a void.
If your body-shelter didn't
guarantee the propagation of men
you might as well not have been born.

To be born a woman is to come to nothing.
A life devoid of yourself
where everyone else—not your heart—
decides or stipulates.

To be born a woman is to be at the bottom
of the well, the abyss, the moat
around the walled city
inhabited by Them, only by Them,
whom you'll have to charm, fool,
serve, sell out to, flatter, humiliate yourself for,
rebel against, swim against the current of, fight,
shout, shout, shout
until you split the stones,
escape through the cracks,

botar el puente levadizo, desmoronar los muros,
ascender el foso, saltar sobre el abismo,
lanzarte sin alas a salvar el precipicio
impulsada por tu propio corazón
sostenida por tus propios pensamientos
hasta librarte del horror al vacío
que tendrás que vencer
sólo con tu voz y tu palabra.

knock down the drawbridge, destroy the walls,
get over the moat, jump the abyss,
throw yourself wingless across the precipice
driven by your own heart
supported by your own thoughts
until you're freed from the horror of the void
you will only defeat
with your voice and your word.

WE TAKE YOU FOR GRANTED
_____
CONTAMOS CON QUE ESTÁS

PARA MI ABUELO VICENTE,
DESDE ENERO HASTA SU MUERTE

I.

Tú y yo poseemos un marco de silencio
que nadie penetra
y en el que sólo platicamos
tú y yo.

Porque del mismo manantial brotamos
del mismo árbol, de la misma piel.
Y en el camino, de nuevo nos encontramos
y nos reconocimos.
Aunque había mucha gente y te llamaban,
tú te quedabas sentado en la vereda y me esperabas.

Era yo muy pequeña cuando me encontraste,
y a tu sombra, fresca como de sauce,
me cobijé y crecí tranquila.
Tus ramas se extendían flexibles como lirios
y detenías las lluvias, los vientos y las fieras.
Sólo la luz entraba filtrada entre tus hojas.

Hoy soy fuerte y a ti
se te han ido las hojas con el viento de Enero.
Pero no te aflijas, que ya he visto retoños
brotar entre tus ramas.
Pasará la sequía y cuando Mayo llegue
tus ramas estarán cubiertas de hojas tiernas.
Y de nuevo habrán lluvias, y sequías y vientos . . .
Pero tu savia es fuerte,
tendrás retoños nuevos,

FOR MY GRANDFATHER VICENTE, FROM JANUARY UNTIL HIS DEATH

I

You and I share a border of silence
no one can penetrate,
and a conversation existing only
between us.

We gush from the same source
the same tree, the same skin.
And a road of new encounters
and recognitions.
Many people were reaching for you and talking,
but you remained seated along the path waiting for me.

I was very small when you found me,
and your shade, like fresh air beneath a willow,
was my shelter while I grew in peace.
Your branches, arched like supple lilies,
kept out the rain, the winds and wild animals.
Only light was permitted to filter through your leaves.

Today I'm strong and you
your leaves have gone wild in January wind.
But don't grieve, I already see sprouts
budding among your branches.
The drought will pass, and when May comes
tender leaves will envelope you.
Then there will be new rains, and droughts and winds . . .
But your sap is vigorous,
there will be new shoots,

y tu sombra, fresca como de sauce,
rumorosa y flexible,
permanecerá viva para siempre.

II.

¿Por qué te fuiste?

Los bambúes que sembraste a la orilla del camino,
los heliotropos y las gardenias preguntan por ti.
Los rosales te esperan y las gencianas dobles.
Los jazmines y las gemelas,
la llama-del-bosque y las acacias,
los mangos-enanos y los guanacastes,
el laurel-de-la-India y los cardoncillos,
todos preguntan que cuándo regresarás.

El chilamate del patio adoquinado
cada día te espera con su sombra abierta
y la pitahaya no quiere florecer hasta que vuelvas.

Desde que te fuiste
las ranas ya no cantan en las noches de lluvia
y las quiebra-plata no brillarán más.

La fuente está oscura y callada,
tu cuarto desierto, tu hamaca vacía,
tu escritorio, tu sombrero, tu capote y tu mochila,
tu machete y tus botas,
todos están quietos y te esperan . . .

¿Por qué te fuiste?
¿Por qué dejaste todo lo que amabas?

¿Por qué?

and your shade, like fresh air beneath a willow,
murmuring and supple,
will live forever.

II.

Why did you leave?

The bamboo you planted along the road,
the heliotropes and gardenias, ask for you.
The rose bushes wait for you, and the double gentians.
The jessamine and Arab jasmine,
the flames-of-the-forest and acacias,
the dwarf mangos and guanacaste trees,
the Indian laurels and milk-thistles,
all ask when you're coming back.

The laurel-leafed figs in the courtyard
long for you each day with their broad shade,
and the tree-cactus doesn't want to bloom until you're here.

Since you've been gone
frogs don't sing in the night rain
and fireflies no longer glow.

The fountain is dark and silent,
your room deserted, hammock empty,
your desk, your hat, your poncho and knapsack,
your machete and boots,
are all quiet with expectation . . .

Why did you leave?
Why did you give up all that you loved?

¿Por qué?

III.

Ahora quisiera regresar —inútilmente—
a los últimos días dolorosos
llenos de medicinas y visitas y voces,
de instrucciones y horarios y angustia contenida.
Y de aquella esperanza —pequeña y persistente—
que ninguno decía, pero que de algún modo
—no me explico por qué—
los dos guardábamos.

Quisiera regresar aún más todavía
a los días en que agarrabas contento tu machete,
y te ibas muy temprano a ver los animales,
y la penca, y todos los detalles de la finca.
Y a la hora del almuerzo nos contabas
de los recién nacidos terneros
de la nueva presa de la finca en Boaco
y de la posible compra de guapotes y camarones
para llenarla.
De las latas de miel que había que embotellar,
y de la siembra de naranjas y mandarinas,
de la cosecha y de las lluvias,
y de la tierra, que tanto amabas
porque tú la habías trabajado con tus manos.
Y después sentados en el corredor
platicábamos viejas historias en el frescor de la tarde.

Pero más que todo eso quisiera
regresar hasta los más antiguos días
aquellos en que me diste el mote de "hoja-chigüe"
—por fregar tanto—
y me dabas volantines en las camas
y por las noches
me hacías ejercicios de lectura en los periódicos.

Y después me acostaba y soñaba los juegos
que juntos jugaríamos la siguiente mañana.

III.

I wish now to return—however uselessly—
to those painful final days
filled with medicine and visitors, the clamor
of instructions, timetables, restrained anguish.
And of a hope, small and persistent,
one we were not speaking of but somehow
—I can't explain—
we held inside.

Even more, I wish to return
to those days you held your machete with contentment,
out early in the morning to check the animals,
the hemp plants, every detail of your land.
And the lunches where you told stories
about newborn calves
and talked about the new dam at your farm in Boaco,
maybe buying freshwater herring and shrimp
to stock it.
The bottling of honey from storage barrels,
planting oranges and mandarins,
the harvest and the rains,
the earth you loved so dearly
because you worked it with your hands.
We'd sit on the verandah afterwards
exchanging old stories in the cool evening air.

But more than anything I wish
to return to those ancient days
when you gave me the nickname "*hoja-chigüe*"*
—for being such a pain-in-the-neck—
and playfully tossed me flying into bed,
and for the nights
you taught me to read the news.

Afterwards, I'd lie there dreaming about the games
we might play together in the morning.

107

IV.

En realidad lo más terrible de tu muerte es
aquello de llegar a la casa y no encontrarte.
Aquella persistencia del vacío
que no importa lo me esfuerce
sé que allí está y que además
nunca habrá manera posible de romperlo.

V.

Hoy regresó la lluvia, la misma lluvia de antes.
El zacate está verde y el camino lodoso.
Y todo como siempre, pero nuevo y distinto,
igual y distinto.

Porque es la antigua lluvia que vuelve
como tú que te fuiste y estás aquí conmigo
(porque se puede estar y no estar al mismo tiempo).
Y has estado siempre y seguirás estando,
como la lluvia de hoy que es de ayer y mañana,
que ha sucedido siempre sin final ni principio,
y nadie sabe cuándo fue el primer aguacero.

IV.

In reality, the worst of your death is
coming home and not finding you there.
That persistent void
which makes all effort irrelevant,
knowing there will always be this thing
never to be recovered from the wreckage.

V.

The rain returned today, the same rain as before.
The hay is green, the road muddy.
Everything's the same as always, but new and different,
the same but different.

It's an ancient rain that returns
like you who went away but are here with me
(because you can be here and not be at the same time).
You have always been the same and always will be,
like today's rain is yesterday's and tomorrow's,
one always following the other without beginning or end,
no one knowing when the first storm hit.

*hoja-chigüe: This untranslatable, affectionate nickname is Nicaraguan for the Sandpaper tree (*Curatella americana*), the leaves of which are used to sand/polish wooden articles or scrub pots and pans—its lilac-colored flowers have an intensely sweet fragrance. The term *"fregar tanto,"* translated as "pain-in-the-neck" literally means "scrub hard," and can also mean "really pester."

AUTORRETRATO

Y heme aquí
    con veintipico a cuestas
determinado el ritmo de mis días

—al tiempo mansamente asida.

(*circa* 1975)

SELF-PORTRAIT

And here I am
      twenty-some years on my shoulders
length and rhythm of my days predetermined

—tamed and clinging to time.

(*circa* 1975)

LA VISITA

Cric-crac-cric-crac-cric-crac... La música de los balancines las acompaña allá, al fondo de esa plática ajena a todos los ruidos: el bullicio de los niños, el trastear de cacharros en la cocina, coches de caballos y carretones. En la sala en penumbra, el rectángulo de luz las enmarca, agobiadas siluetas oscuras, aún más delgadas en la intensa claridad que las aparta de los demás que sólo podemos verlas en ruinas: cegatas y desdentadas. Ellas fueron dos muchachas rubias y de ojos azules: la una, recién llegada de Hamburgo y Nueva Orléans; la otra, su prima que la recibe en Masaya. Parlotean, se intercambian confidencias, inocentes secretos y complicidades, envueltas en un tiempo desconocido, atmósfera sepia, perdida para siempre en cofres y daguerrotipos extraviados.

THE VISIT

Cric-crac-cric-crac-cric-crac . . . rocking chair music accompanies them in the depths of a conversation alien to all the noises: the racket of children, banging of pots and pans in the kitchen, horse carriages, carts. In the half-lit living room, a rectangle of light frames their stooped, dark silhouettes, even thinner looking in the intense clarity that separates them from the rest of us, who can only can see them in ruins: blind and toothless. They were once two blonde, blue-eyed girls: one just arrived from Hamburg and New Orleans, the other, her cousin, receiving her in Masaya. They chatter on, exchanging confidences, innocent secrets and complicity, enveloped in an unknown time, a sepia atmosphere gone forever in trunks and misplaced daguerreotypes.

VIEJA TÍA ABUELA

... mi infancia feliz despierta, como una lágrima en mí
Fernando Pessoa

Qué angustia escucharla arrastrar los pies.
Ella, tan ágil,
   subía y bajaba presurosa
   por la vieja casona.

Con dificultad lee mis poemas.
Ella, que entre oficio y oficio
tejía y bordaba primores
en sobrecamas, sábanas, fundas,
   tapetes y manteles.

Viuda que desquitó con su trabajo:
contaba la ropa,
   despachaba la leche de la hacienda,
gobernaba la despensa, recibía los víveres,
   disponía las compras del mercado.

Hermana mayor desde jovencita,
   cuidando a las menores
y atendiendo a los varones, mayores que ella.

Nacida en Hamburgo en 1900,
una fotografía de Rudolf Henkel
   (Hamburg Uhlenhorst
   Hofweg 50)
muestra niña y muñeca
   de bucles rubios y ojos azules
inmersas en vuelos y encajes,
   coronadas de lazos.

OLD GREAT-AUNT

... my happy childhood comes to me as a tear
Fernando Pessoa

What an anguish to hear her drag her feet.
She, so agile,
    who went rushing up and down
    throughout the ancient manor house

She reads my poems with difficulty now.
She who between chore and chore
knitted and embroidered exquisite
bedspreads, pillowcases, sheets,
    doilies and tablecloths.

Widow who earned her keep with hard work:
tallied laundry for the household,
    dispensed morning milk from the family farm to the
        neighborhood,
ruled the pantry, received provisions,
    detailed shopping lists for the market.

An older sister from girlhood,
    she took care of her younger sisters
and looked after her older brothers.

Born in Hamburg in 1900,
a photo by one Rudolf Henkel
    (Hamburg Uhlenhorst
    Hofweg 50)
shows a little girl and doll
    both with blonde ringlets and blue eyes
immersed in ruffles and lace,
    crowned with bows.

Varias generaciones de sobrinos, criados por ella.
(Yo, la más desamparada.)
Guardiana de mis sueños,
    custodia de mis fiebres y terrores,
Ana María Gámez, vieja tía-abuela,
    que no se me muera.

Several generations of nieces and nephews were raised by her.
　　(I, the most vulnerable.)
Guardian of my dreams,
　　custodian of my fevers and terrors,
Ana María Gámez, old great-aunt,
　　may she never die.

HERMANAS

A: Milena y María José

Entre las rejas, esplendorosos racimos de heliotropos.
Un aroma tierno inunda el porche
como piel recién nacida.

No sé de qué hablamos, por qué nos reímos,
y de repente todo se vuelve puro:
una muñeca vestida de azul,
tafetanes susurrantes bajo el vestido de organdí,
fragancia vegetal de azucenas,
dulzura de cera ardiente en la capilla iluminada,
aleteo de palomas desde un tejado húmedo
                              de musgo y líquenes.

Materia primigenia, carne original
antes de convertirse en nuestros cuerpos,
sangre común antes de ser repartida
                              entre nosotras tres.
Momento de plenitud, instante diáfano
en que padre y madre nos soñaron
abrasados por el fuego de un sol de ámbar.

SISTERS

To Milena and María José

Between the grillwork, magnificent clusters of heliotropes.
A tender perfume floods the porch
like that of a newborn's skin

I don't know what we're discussing, or why we're laughing,
but suddenly everything becomes pure:
a doll dressed in blue,
the rustling of taffeta beneath an organdy dress,
the vegetal fragrance of lilies,
the sweetness of burning wax in the illuminated chapel,
pigeon wings flapping from a damp roof
                              of moss and lichens.

Primal matter, original flesh
before transforming into our bodies,
common blood before it's shared
                              among the three of us.
A moment of plenitude, a crystalline instant
in which father and mother dreamed of us
scorched and embraced by the blaze of an amber sun.

CONTAMOS CON QUE ESTÁS

A mi madre

Seguimos mirándote
cristalizada en un tiempo sin tiempo.
De pronto, me choca tu cabello blanco
(¿cuándo perdió su esplendor de caoba?).
Te veo casualmente cambiándote de ropa
y me conmuevo:
ahora tu cuerpo es más pequeño y frágil.
(¿Qué crisis enfrentaste calladamente
en tantos años de soledad y viudez?)
Pero son momentos, sólo momentos
que luego olvidamos
cada quién en el trajín de la vida.

Contamos con que estás,
te visitamos de vez en cuando
y cruzamos —como pájaros—
breves palabras al vuelo.
Y seguimos posponiendo el verdadero
encuentro, la conversación definitiva,
como si la vida durara para siempre,
como si no pudiera
terminarse todo hoy mismo.

WE TAKE YOU FOR GRANTED

To my mother

We see you
crystallized in a time without time.
Suddenly, I'm shocked by your white hair
(when did it lose that mahogany splendor?).
By chance I see you changing your clothes
and it moves me:
now your body is smaller and fragile.
(What crises have you faced in silence
through so many years of loneliness and widowhood?)
But these are moments, only moments
we soon forget
in the rush of life.

We take you for granted,
visit you once in a while
and pass—like birds—
brief words brushing the air.
And we keep putting off the true
encounter, that definitive conversation,
as if life will last forever,
as if it couldn't
all just end today.

QUERIDA TÍA CHOFI

A: *Adilia Moncada*

No eras la tía Chofi del poema de Jaime Sabines,
pero también te llamabas Sofía, Chofi.
Vos, la rebelde desde chiquita,
la que se casó contra todo el mundo
pero con su hombre. Aunque la vida
después resultara un purgatorio e infierno
hasta que Guillermo terminó desnucándose borracho
para tu descanso. Y concluiste
otro capítulo de tu vida
que yo te escuchaba contar, fascinada,
mientras hacías escarchas de azúcar de colores
que secabas al sol en láminas de vidrio.

Artesana, Imaginera, Panadera, Decoradora,
poblaste tu mundo de enanos, Blancanieves,
Cenicientas, niñas de 15 años,
parejas de Primera Comunión, casamientos,
tiernos de Bautizo,
entre tules, perlas, filigranas,
ramilletes, cintas y lazos de pastillaje.

Los sacuanjoches sacados de panas de agua
se convertían en tus manos en coronas,
diademas y cetros frescos
—efímeros símbolos de efímeros reinados.
Los mediodías eran la penumbra de tu cuarto
contra el solazo. Tu aposento lleno de pinceles,
óleos, moldes de yeso,
caballetes, lienzos, bastidores,
santos de bulto a medio retocar,
y en medio del caos, tu cama eternamente desarreglada.

MY DEAR AUNT CHOFI

for Adilia Moncada

You weren't the Aunt Chofi of Jaime Sabines' poem,
but you were also named Sofía, Chofi.
You, rebellious from childhood,
who married her man against the wishes
of everyone in the world. Even though life
later turned into purgatory then hell
until Guillermo got drunk and broke his neck
and gave you some rest. And so you wrapped up
another chapter in your life,
which I listened to you retell, fascinated,
while you made colored sugar candy
dried on sheets of glass in the sun.

Craftswoman, holy image maker, baker, decorator,
you peopled your world with dwarfs, Snow Whites,
Cinderellas, fifteen-year-old girls,
First Communion couples, marriages,
baptized infants,
in the midst of tulle, pearls, filigree,
bouquets, ribbons, and swirls of frosting.

Sacuanjoche flowers scooped from water tubs
became crowns in your hands,
diadems, and fresh scepters
—ephemeral symbols of ephemeral kingdoms.
Middays meant the shade of your bedroom
against scorching sun. Your room filled with paintbrushes,
oils, plaster molds,
easels, canvases, frames,
half-finished figures of saints,
and in the middle of the chaos, your perpetually unmade bed.

Habladora, conversadora, platicabas mientras ibas
fumando cigarrillos,
encendiendo uno con la colilla del otro
hasta dejar tu cuarto como un cenicero lleno
de colillas retorcidas y fragante a tazas de café,
miel, azúcar, harina, claras de huevo,
trementina, aceite de linaza,
sábanas viejas.

Amazona admirable en tus fantásticas hazañas:
amarraste al ebrio de tu marido,
te amaste con el primer Gurú legítimo de la India
que pasó por Managua.
Curandera, hacías medicinas, jarabes y pócimas terribles
que nos obligabas a beber
contra todas las enfermedades posibles.

Recorrías Managua bajo aquel solazo
con tu cartera repleta de chunches,
el pelo alborotado,
y la eterna brasa entre los labios.

Qué necesidad, qué desgracia no ayudaste:
Partera, Enfermera,
alistabas muertos, atendías borrachos,
defendías causas perdidas desde siempre,
y en todas las discusiones familiares
gobernaba tu figura desgarbada.

Siempre en tránsito, viviste
en cuartos alquilados,
te salvaste de milagro en los terremotos,
y cualquier persona soportó cualquier barbaridad tuya.
Te peleaste hasta con la guardia
y fuiste a parar al exilio de México.

Great talker, conversationalist, you chattered
while smoking cigarettes,
lighting one with the tail end of another
until your room ended up like an ashtray
full of crushed butts and fragrant cups of coffee,
honey, sugar, flour, egg whites,
turpentine, linseed oil,
stale bedsheets.

Admirable Amazon of fantastic deeds:
you tied your drunken husband to the bed,
you fell in love with the first legitimate Indian Guru
who passed through Managua.
Curandera, you brewed medicines, syrups and terrible potions
you made us drink
to guard against all possible sickness.

You ran around Managua in the blazing sun
with a purse full of thingamajigs,
hair disheveled,
that eternal ember between your lips.

What necessity or misfortune did you ever miss:
midwife, nurse,
you took care of drunks, prepared the dead,
defended lost causes all your life,
and every family discussion
was ruled by your awkward figure.

Always in transit,
you lived in rented rooms,
miraculously survived earthquakes,
and everyone had to endure your rudeness.
You even argued with the National Guard
then fled to exile in Mexico.

A veces, con tus manos pequeñitas y regordetas
de puntas afiladas, como manos de bebé
o como palmeritas de abanico en miniatura,
te arreglabas el pelo entrecano
con una onda sobre la frente
y en ese gesto rápido, fugazmente
se vislumbraba tu antigua gracia.

Porque un día de verdad que fuiste hermosa,
morena y altiva.
Nada tenía que ver esa joven con vos misma,
Oveja Negra, Paja en ojos ajenos,
Vergüenza de tu única hija
—que a pulso enviaste a estudiar a México—
y de allí saltó a Pittsburgh, a New York,
y recorrió Europa acumulando becas
y títulos académicos
con nostalgias de supuestos linajes
para borrarte, para no verte,
para no tener que sufrirte.
¡Ah!, pero vos te llenabas la boca con su nombre.

La mañana antes de tu muerte
estuviste igual que siempre, gritona y bocatera,
sólo que te quejaste
de mucho malestar en los riñones.
(Tu hija supo la noticia en Buenos Aires.)

Vos que me contabas de tus trances en el espejo
tus reencarnaciones
—múltiples vidas de las que recordabas
incontables anécdotas:
en una de tus vidas fuiste una niña que murió
recién nacida, en otra, un hombre aventurero . . .

Sometimes, your tiny plump hands with pointed finger tips,
like the hands of a baby
or like palm trees fanned out in miniature,
arranged your graying hair
in a wave over your forehead
with a quick gesture that revealed
a fleeting glimpse of your former charms.

Once you were truly beautiful,
dark and proud.
But that young girl you were has nothing to do with you now,
black sheep, speck in the eye,
shame of your only daughter
—for whom you slaved so you could send her to study in Mexico,
from where she leapt to Pittsburgh, New York,
traveling all over Europe accumulating scholarships
and academic degrees
yearning for so-called nobility
to erase you, make you invisible,
not have to put up with you.
Ah! but your mouth was filled with her name.

The morning before your death
you were the same as ever, loud-mouthed and hollering,
but complained of discomfort in your kidneys.
(Your daughter heard the news in Buenos Aires.)

You told me about your trances in the mirror
your reincarnations
—multiple lives from which you remembered
innumerable anecdotes:
in one of them you were a newborn child that died,
in another an adventurer . . .

¿En qué vida estás ahora
que ya no te llamás Sofía,
      Sabia, Sabiduría,
ahora que te llamás huesos, madera desvencijada,
podredumbre, tierra vegetal,
humus, fosa, oscuridad,
           nada?

Ahora que ya no estás, que ya no existís,
quizás te reconozcás
          en este espejo.

What life are you in now,
now that your name isn't Sofía (Wisdom),
                Sabia (Wise), Sabiduría (Wisdom),
now that your name is bones, rotten wood,
putrefaction, vegetal earth,
humus, grave, darkness,
                                nothing?

Now that you are not, now that you do not exist,
perhaps you recognize yourself
                        in this mirror.

The first line refers to the poem "Tía Chofi" by Mexican poet Jaime
Sabines; *sacuanjoche* is the national flower of Nicaragua; a *curandera*
is a folk healer or medicine woman.

DIVISAR LA MUERTE

Cuando finalmente mi tía abuela
en penosa ascensión al Mirador de Catarina
logró contemplar la laguna de Apoyo
—inmenso y límpido iris bajo el domo del cielo—
sus ojos estaban llorosos detrás de los gruesos lentes.

Se quedó silenciosa un momento, y después preguntó:
¿La muerte será como este cielo azul, combo, infinito?

DISCERNING DEATH

When my great-aunt finally
and painfully climbed Catarina Vista
to gaze out over Apoyo Lagoon
—vast, transparent iris beneath sky's dome—
her eyes grew tearful behind thick glasses.

She was silent a while, then asked:
Will death be like the curved blue infinity of this sky?

FRAGMENTOS DE LA MEMORIA

Retazos de melodías y canciones,
olores sepias y polvosos del verano,
húmedas fragancias verdes,
cabellos empapados,
risas infantiles ondeando sobre los charcos,
camisa de dril de un abuelo, aroma de su mejilla,
ordeños de madrugada, leche, espuma tibia,
aire de mañana clara, sangre fresca y dorada de naranjas,
paseos bajo la luna, conversaciones,
voces perdidas que regresan en sueños,
pecho balsámico, mano amorosa sobre la frente enfebrecida,
trozos de vidas dispersas,
espejo despedazado de mi vida,
fragmentos de la memoria.

MEMORY FRAGMENTS

Shreds of song and melody,
sepia summer dust aroma,
wet green fragrance,
drenched hair,
children's laughter rippling from puddles,
grandfather's workshirt, scent of his cheek,
milkings at dawn, milk, warm froth,
bright morning air, fresh golden blood of oranges,
moonlight strolls, conversations,
lost voices returning in dreams,
soothing breast, loving hand on a fevered head,
pieces of scattered lives,
broken mirror of my life,
fragments of memory.

ABUELO DESPUÉS DE LA MUERTE

Nadie entendió mi obstinación
en sostenerle la barbilla.

¿Quién iba a entender el diálogo secreto
de mis manos
al contacto de la amada arquitectura
de su rostro?

¿Quién habría sabido qué universo incorrupto,
qué desprendido amor, qué celeste alegría
palpaba con mis dedos
en su piel aún tibia,
en sus labios violáceos,
en su mandíbula rígida?

(¿Quién entendería nunca?)
(¡Jamás entenderían!)

GRANDFATHER AFTER DEATH

No one understood my stubbornness
about holding his chin until his mouth stayed closed.

Who would have understood the secret dialogue
of my hands
touching the beloved architecture
of his face?

Who could have known what uncorrupted universe,
what open-handed love, what celestial joy
I sensed with my fingers
in his still warm flesh,
in his purpled lips,
in his stiffened jaw?

(Who would have ever understood?)
(No one would ever!)

LINAJE

Pregunto por las mujeres de mi casa.

Desde niña supe la historia del bisabuelo:
Científico, diplomático, liberal, político,
padre de prole numerosa y distinguida.

¿Y Doña Isolina Reyes, casada con él desde
los quince años hasta su muerte, cuál fue su historia?

Mi abuelo materno se graduó *Cum Laude*
en la Universidad de Filadelfia
y aún se conserva su tesis, fechada en 1900.
Dirigió la construcción de kilómetros de vía férrea,
y sólo la muerte repentina truncó su sueño
de extender el ferrocarril hasta la Costa Atlántica.
Nueve hijos e hijas lo lloraron.

¿Y su esposa Rudecinda, que parió esos hijos,
los cuidó y amamantó, qué sé de ella?

Pregunto por las mujeres de mi casa.

Mi otro abuelo era un patriarca
cuya sombra amparaba a la familia entera
(incluidos cuñados, primos, parientes lejanos, amigos,
conocidos, y hasta enemigos).
Empeñó su vida en ampliar un patrimonio
que todos dilapidaron después de su muerte.

¿Y a mi abuela Ilse, ya viuda y despojada
que le quedó, sino morirse?

Pregunto por mí, por ellas, por las mujeres de mi casa.

LINEAGE

I ask about the women of my house.

Since childhood I've known the history of my great-grandfather:
Scientist, diplomat, liberal, politician,
father of numerous and distinguished offspring.

But Doña Isolina Reyes, married to him
from fifteen until death, what was her history?

My maternal grandfather graduated Cum Laude
from the University of Philadelphia
and his thesis, dated 1900, is still preserved.
He oversaw the construction of many kilometers of train track,
and only sudden death shattered his dream
of extending the railroad all the way to the Atlantic Coast.
Nine sons and daughters mourned him.

And his wife Rudecinda, who gave birth to those children,
cared for and breast-fed them, what do I know of her?

I ask about the women of my house.

My other grandfather was a patriarch
who sheltered the entire family with his shade
(including in-laws, cousins, distant relatives, friends,
acquaintances, even enemies).
He committed his life to expanding a patrimony
everyone squandered after his death.

And my grandmother Ilse, his dispossessed widow,
what was left for her but to die?

I ask for me, for them, for the women of my house.

DETALLE

Cuando por encima estemos
          ya del tiempo,
algún detalle
          permanezca.

Tan leves son nuestros pies,
          tan breve el paso.

DETAIL

When it's all
            over,
let's trust some detail
         remains.

So light our footsteps,
         so brief the trip.

URGENT MESSAGE TO MY MOTHER

MENSAJE URGENTE A MI MADRE

MENSAJE URGENTE A MI MADRE

Todas íbamos a ser reinas,
y de verídico reinar;
pero ninguna ha sido reina
ni en Arauco ni en Copán ...

Gabriela Mistral

Fuimos educadas para la perfección:
Para que nada fallara y se cumpliera
nuestra suerte de princesa-de-cuentos infantiles.

¡Cómo nos esforzamos, ansiosas por demostrar
que eran ciertas las esperanzas tanto tiempo atesoradas!

Pero envejecieron nuestros vestidos de novia
y nuestros corazones, exhaustos,
últimos sobrevivientes de la contienda.
Hemos tirado al fondo de vetustos armarios
velos amarillentos, azahares marchitos.
Ya nunca más seremos sumisas ni perfectas.

Perdón, madre, por las impertinencias
de gallinas viejas y copetudas
que sólo saben cacarearte bellezas
de hijas dóciles y anodinas.

Perdón, por no habernos quedado
donde nos obligaban la tradición
y el buen gusto.

URGENT MESSAGE TO MY MOTHER

We were all going to be queens,
and truly reign;
but no one has been a queen
neither in Arauco nor Copán...

Gabriela Mistral

We were educated for perfection:
so nothing would fail and we'd achieve
our storybook-princess fate.

How hard we tried, eager to prove
those hopes, treasured so long, were true!

But our wedding gowns grew old
and our hearts exhausted,
last survivors of the battle.
We've tossed yellowed veils and withered
orange blossoms to the back of ancient armoires.*
We will never again be submissive or perfect.

Sorry, mother, for the impertinence
of those stuck-up old hens who know
only how to cluck with praise
for bland, docile daughters.

Sorry, for not staying
where tradition and good taste
obliged us to stay.

Por atrevernos a ser nosotras mismas
al precio de destrozar
todos tus sueños.

For daring to be ourselves
at the cost of destroying
all your dreams.

In Latin American and Spanish tradition, orange blossoms symbolize purity and
are part of a bride's wedding attire in crowns and bouquets.

ERA UNA ESCUADRA DESPERDIGADA

(Septiembre de 1978)

Nadie quería cruzar aquel campo quemado.
(Las cenizas plateadas y algún destello rojo
        de las últimas brasas).
Te tiraste de primero y tu cuerpo se miraba oscuro
        contra lo blanco.
Escondidos en el monte, los demás esperábamos
        verte alcanzar la orilla
para irnos cruzando.

Como en cámara lenta lo recuerdo:
El terreno inclinado, resbaloso, caliente,
la mano agarrada al fusil
        el olor a quemado.
El ruido de las hélices,
de vez en cuando, ráfagas.

Tus botas se enterraban en lo blando
y levantabas un vaho blanquecino
        a cada paso.
(Debe haber sido un tiempo
    que se nos hizo largo)

Todos los compañeros, Dionisio, te mirábamos,
nuestros pechos latiendo inútilmente
        bajo la luna llena.

146

A SCATTERED SQUAD

(September 1978)

No one wanted to cross that burned field.
(Silvery ashes and a red glimmer
             of the last embers).
You jumped out first and your body looked dark
             against the white.
Hidden at the edge of the forest, the rest of us waited for you
             to reach the other side
before crossing.

I remember it like a slow motion film:
the sloping terrain, slippery, hot,
hand gripping a gun,
             the smell of burning.
Helicopter sound,
sporadic machine gun fire.

Your boots sank in the softness
and you let out a whitish breath
             with each step.
(Time must have
             dragged for us)

All the comrades, Dionisio, were watching you,
our hearts beating futilely
             beneath the full moon.

VUELVO A SER YO MISMA

Cuando entro con mis hijos a su casa
vuelvo a ser yo misma.
Desde su mecedora ella
nos siente llegar y alza la cabeza.
La conversación no es como antes,
ella está a punto de irse.
Pero llego a esconder mi cabeza
en su regazo, a sentarme a sus pies,
y ella me contempla
desde mi paraíso perdido
donde mi rostro era otro, que sólo ella conoce.
Rostro por instantes recuperado
cada vez más débilmente
en su iris celeste desvaído
y en sus pupilas que lo guardan ciegamente.

I COME BACK TO MYSELF

When I enter her house with my kids
I come back to myself.
From her rocking chair she
senses us and raises her head.
Our conversations aren't like before—
she's on the verge of death.
But I go there to sit at her feet
with my head in her lap,
and she sees me
from a lost paradise
where my face was different, one only she knows now.
A face recovered in moments
a little weaker each time
by her faded blue eyes
and pupils that guard it fiercely.

HIJA

Como hojita de sauce
                    o de bambú,
te me pegás
buscando mi sombra
                    frágil.

DAUGHTER

Like a fresh willow
              or bamboo leaf,
you cling to me
in search of my fragile
              shadow.

ESPEJO DE MANO

Después de tantos años,
mi abuela Ilse regresa
con sus asombrados ojos
oscuros y tristones, y se asoma
     —grácil Narciso—
a su pequeño estanque de plata,
a su óvalo mágico,
a su luna de cristal cortado,
ocupando este rostro
cada vez más suyo
               y menos mío.

HAND MIRROR

After so many years,
my grandmother Ilse returns,
dark eyes delighted
and sorrowful she leans
      —graceful Narcissus—
over her tiny silver pond,
her magic oval,
cut glass moon,
taking the place of this face
more and more hers
             than mine.

MUJER PARA LA ESPECIE

A: María Denise

Desde los estantes polvosos
tus muñecas, nostálgicas, te observan:
cuánto has cambiado.
Abandonas la infancia sin señales de duelo.

Ávida de ti misma
en la íntima turbación del baño
descubres cada día tu cuerpo florecido.

Tu padre reclama tu aire ausente.

Tus hermanos menores no entienden nada:
los prolongados encierros / la soledad.

Y tú, te asqueaste la primera vez que tu sangre
manchó tu ropa.

Apenas puedo compañarte,
apenas puedo explicarte
que otro será tu tiempo / otra tu historia.
Que ahora recomienza tu historia:
niña, adolescente, mujer para la especie.

WOMAN FOR THE SPECIES

For María Denise

Your dolls watch you nostalgically
from their dusty shelves:
how you've changed!
You've left childhood behind without a sign of mourning.

Eager to be yourself
in the intimate confusion of the bath
you discover your body blooming each day.

Your father complains of your distracted look.

Your little brothers understand nothing:
the prolonged seclusions / the solitude.

And you, you were nauseous the first time your blood
stained your clothes.

I can hardly keep up with you,
barely explain
that yours will be another era / another history.
That your history begins now:
girl child, teenager, woman for the species.

HOSPITALIZACIÓN DE EMERGENCIA

Rebotaba el sol sobre la grama china.
Semáforos, intersecciones casi desiertas.

Dimos vuelta y entramos por el portón.

Pasillos verdes, ladrillos al rojo intenso,
seres ingrávidos, blancos, silenciosos,
habitación en penumbra, susurros,
reflejos, presión, temperatura, signos vitales.
Escucho nombres: Sandra, Carmen, Marta, Idania . . .

Análisis de sangre, orina, rayos X, scanner,
agujas, suero, analgésicos.
Otra vez susurros, susurros, susurros,
un foco, oscuridad, silencio.

. . . Mis últimos recuerdos
si la meningitis hubiera sido fulminante.

RUSHED TO THE HOSPITAL

Sunlight ricocheted off Chinese grass.
Stoplights and intersections nearly deserted.

We turned and entered the gate.

Hallways green, hot-red floor tiles,
floating beings, white and silent,
a half-lit room, whispers,
reflexes, blood pressure, temperature, vital signs.
I hear names: Sandra, Carmen, Marta, Idania . . .

Blood and urine tests, X-rays, scanner,
hypodermic needles, intravenous serum, analgesics.
Once again whispers, whispers, whispers,
a spotlight, darkness, silence.

. . . My last memories
had the meningitis been deadly.

DÍA DE LAS MADRES

A mi hija e hijos

No dudo que les hubiera gustado tener
una linda mamá de anuncio comercial:
       con marido adorable y niños felices.
Siempre aparece risueña —y si algún día llora—
lo hace una vez apagados reflectores y cámaras
y con el rostro limpio de maquillaje.

Pero ya que nacieron de mí, debo decirles:
Desde que era pequeña como ustedes
ansiaba ser yo misma —y para una mujer eso es difícil—
(Hasta mi Ángel Guardián renunció a cuidarme
cuando lo supo).

No puedo asegurarles que conozco bien el rumbo.
Muchas veces me equivoco,
y mi vida más bien ha sido como una dolorosa travesía
vadeando escollos, sorteando tempestades,
desoyendo fantasmales sirenas que me invitan al pasado,
sin brújula ni bitácora adecuadas
que me indiquen la ruta.

Pero avanzo. Avanzo aferrada a la esperanza
de algún puerto lejano
al que ustedes, hijos míos —estoy segura—
arribarán una mañana
—después de consumado
mi naufragio.

MOTHER'S DAY

For my children

No doubt you would have liked
one of those pretty mothers in the TV ads
       with an adoring husband and happy children.
She's always cheerful—and if she ever cries
it's when the spotlights and cameras have snapped off
and she's removed her make-up.

But since you were born from me, I have to tell you:
Ever since I was a child like you
I've wanted to be myself—and for a woman that's difficult—
(Even my Guardian Angel refused to protect me
when she found out).

I can't tell you I know exactly where I'm going.
I often make mistakes,
and my life has been a painful voyage
navigating reefs, winding through storms,
ignoring ghostly sirens luring me back to the past,
without a compass or the right chart
to show me the way.

But I continue, continue clinging to the hope
of some distant port
where you, my children—I am sure—
will land one morning
—after I am
shipwrecked.

ARRURRÚ PARA UNA MUERTA RECIÉN NACIDA

¿Cómo hubiera sido tu sonrisa?
¿Qué habrías aprendido a decir primero?
¡Tanta esperanza para nada!
Tuve que secar mis pechos que te esperaban.

Una fotografía apresurada
insinúa tu limpio perfil,
la breve boca.
Pero no puedo recordar cómo eras,
cómo habrías sido.

Tan viva te sentí, dándote vueltas
protegida en mi vientre.
Ahora me despierto estremecida
en medio de la noche
—hueco el vientre—
y me aferro a un impreciso primer llanto
que escuché anestesiada
en el quirófano.

LULLABY FOR A NEWBORN GIRL WHO DIED

How would your smile have been?
What would you have learned to say first?
So much hope for nothing!
I had to milk my breasts that were waiting for you.

A hurried photograph
hints at your fresh profile,
the brief mouth.
But I can't remember how you were,
how you would have been.

You were so alive moving around
protected in my womb.
Now I wake up shuddering
in the middle of the night
—a hollow womb—
clinging to a vague first cry
I heard, anesthetized
in the operating room.

CAMPO ARRASADO

La maleta de su ropita que guardé con tanto
                                    cuidado,
la niña que cruza la calle en brazos de su
                                    madre,
o la visión efímera de una mujer preñada
                                    esperando el bus.

Cualquier encuentro / chispa / desata la
                                    hoguera
de este desprevenido corazón: zacate seco,
                                    yesca
que se reduce a cenizas humeantes, a
                                    campo arrasado.

RAZED FIELD

The suitcase of her little clothes I kept with so much
care,
a baby girl crossing the street in her mother's
arms,
the ephemeral vision of a pregnant woman
waiting for a bus.

Any encounter/ spark / triggers
the bonfire
of this off guard heart: this dry grass,
this tinder
that's reduced to smoking ash, a
razed field.

EL ROSTRO DE LOS MUERTOS

Es vano intento disfrazar el gesto.
La piedad se impone ante
la insistencia de los deudos:

¿Verdad que parece que se va a despertar?
¿Ya la viste qué linda quedó?

Y echamos el obligado vistazo al horror:
caras de muñecos o payasos tétricos.

No es la mascarilla de mosaicos de jade,
ni la momia en decoroso lienzo:
la faz cubierta con su retrato en vida.

Tampoco el sarcófago labrado
con deidades del Hades o del Averno,
ni la olla cineraria del Mictlán
o la hermosa urna de terracota.

Nuestros antepasados temían
y veneraban como a dioses a sus muertos.

Acababa de expirar mi abuelo
y ya era otro: Yo lo ví
afilado y translúcido en atroz quietud.

No pude mirar a mi hija. Sólo
la imagino como un heliotropo yacente.

Mi tía más amada era la angustia inmóvil:
Su viejo pecho hinchado por la última asfixia.

THE FACE OF THE DEAD

It's a vain attempt to disguise the expression.
Mercy is imperative considering
the insistent family of the deceased:

Doesn't it seem like he's going to wake up?
Did you see how beautiful she looks?

And we throw an obligatory glance at the horror:
Faces of gloomy dolls or gloomy clowns.

It's not a death mask of mosaic jade,
nor a mummy wrapped in respectable cloth,
face covered with a portrait from life.

It's not a carved sarcophagus
with deities of Hades or the afterworld,
nor a Mictlán funerary pot
or splendid terra-cotta urn.

Our ancestors feared
and venerated their dead as if they were gods.

As soon as my grandfather died
he was already someone else: I saw him,
features sharpened and translucent in atrocious stillness.

I was unable to see my infant daughter. I just
imagined her as a recumbent heliotrope.

My most beloved aunt was a motionless anguish:
Her old chest swollen by the final asphyxiation.

Inútiles colorines o coloretes.
Semblantes abandonados, vacíos de vida
trascienden sus propios rasgos;
se transforman en otros, distintos de ellos mismos.
Ya no nos pertenecen.

Rostros inviolados, sacrosantos,
tallados por la mano de la Muerte.

Useless bright colors or rouges.
Deserted faces, drained of life
transcend their own features;
transformed into others, distinct from themselves.
They are not ours anymore.

Untouchable, sacred faces
sculpted by the hand of death.

ESPEJISMO

Siempre pensamos, ahora será distinto.
Y volvemos a creer.

De nuevo es bello el mundo. El secreto
oscuro del amor invade el cuerpo. Todos perciben
el resplandor del rostro.

Y la certeza de reposar —al fin— en algún pecho:
besos, manos entrelazadas, brazos,
cuerpos que se confunden, roces húmedos.

Espejismo que nos impide salir de este desierto.

MIRAGE

We always think, this time will be different.
And we want to believe it.

The world becomes beautiful. Love's dark
secrets invade the body. Everyone can tell
by your radiant face.

And the certainty of resting—at last—upon that breast:
kisses, hands entwined, arms,
bodies jumbled together, the steamy coupling.

All a mirage that keeps us from escaping this desert.

NOVELLA

Una mujer se casó, tuvo hijos
y se empeñó en ser feliz.

Hasta que un día
(nunca se sabe cuándo, pero sucede)
escudriñó su corazón a fondo:

Palpó las cicatrices:
comprobó los estragos,
la desolación,
los esfuerzos estériles,
la ruina.

Cuanto tenía que llorar, lloró.

Hizo acopio de fuerzas:
juntó a sus hijos,
empacó unas pocas cosas,
puso a flote su barco,
levó anclas,
zarpó.

NOVELLA

A woman got married, had kids
and made every effort to be happy.

Then one day
(you never know when, but it happens)
she searched her heart to its depths.

She felt the scars:
discovered ravages,
devastation,
fruitless efforts,
ruins.

Whatever she had to cry, she cried.

She mustered all her strength:
got her kids together,
packed a few things,
set her ship afloat,
weighed anchor,
and sailed on.

PARA ENTRAR AL MUNDO

En esa casa habita la miseria.
Conozco a la mujer que vive en ella.
Juntas jugamos
en una infancia que destruyó la vida.

Paso de largo.
No me atrevo a tocar
la desgastada puerta
que guarda el interior oscuro y sórdido
del mundo,
tras las paredes ciegas,
cuarteadas de cal
y sol.

TO ENTER THE WORLD

Misfortune inhabits that house.
I know the woman who lives there.
We played together
in a childhood destroyed by life.

I go right past.
I don't dare knock
on the worn-out door
guarding the dark, squalid interior
of that world
behind blind walls
of crackled whitewash
and sun.

BALANCE FINAL

Ella se llevó:
su ropa, sus libros
y algunos objetos personales.

A él le quedó:
la casa y su mobiliario,
el patio y sus árboles.
Y el jardín, que ella cuidaba.

En fin, él se quedó con todo
menos los niños,
que se fueron con ella
a molestar a otra parte.

FINAL BALANCE

She took:
her clothes, her books
and some personal objects.

He got:
the house and its contents,
the patio and its trees.
And the garden she tended.

In brief, he kept everything
minus the children,
who left with her
to make trouble elsewhere.

AMIGAS / HERMANAS

A: Marta Zamora Llanes

Nada sucedió como lo habíamos previsto.

Pero estábamos recién llegadas a la vida
como a una gran ciudad.
Aturdidas por el bullicio de la multitud.

(Eramos como garzas a la vera de un río.
Como heliotropos radiantes en la primera lluvia.
Un campo de algodón bañado por la luna.)

¿Cuándo fue que la Muerte empezó a visitarnos?

¿En qué momento, a cada una
por fin, nos alcanzó el desastre?

¿Cómo sobrevivimos a la devastación?

No lo sabemos. Cada quién hizo lo que pudo.
En la tierra arrasada quedaron los escombros
que hemos dejado atrás.

Pero a veces, sin quererlo, de pronto recordamos
que alguna vez las ruinas fueron antiguos reinos.

—Espejismos de reinos para el alma desierta.

FRIENDS / SISTERS

For Marta Zamora Llanes

Nothing happened the way we thought it would.

Then again, we'd just arrived to life
as to a big city.
Bewildered by the hustle bustle of the crowd.

(We were like herons on a riverbank.
Radiant heliotropes in first rain.
Cotton fields bathed by the moon.)

When was it Death began to visit us?

At what moment, one by one,
did disaster finally catch up?

And how did we survive the devastation?

Who knows. We each did what we could.
The rubble we left behind
was scattered on scorched earth.

But sometimes, without warning, we suddenly recall
the ruins were ancient kingdoms once.

—Mirage kingdoms for a deserted heart.

MEMORIA

Pudimos no conocernos, pero nos conocimos.

La memoria cubrirá con su pátina de oro
este breve momento de nuestras vidas
que en sus distintos trayectos
apenas se tocaron. Y ahora regresan
otra vez a sus órbitas.

Y más que la memoria, guardará el corazón
nuestras conversaciones. La intimidad construida
a punta de palabras acrisoladas
hasta volverlas puras.

MEMORY

We might not have known each other, but do.

Memory will add a gold patina
to this moment
our lives touched slightly
in different trajectories
then returned to their own orbits.

More than memory, the heart will guard
our conversations, intimacy
made of words melted
in a crucible until pure.

CELEBRACIÓN DEL CUERPO

Amo este cuerpo mío que ha vivido la vida,
su contorno de ánfora, su suavidad de agua,
el borbotón de cabellos que corona mi cráneo,
la copa de cristal del rostro, su delicada base
que asciende pulcra desde hombros y clavículas.

Amo mi espalda pringada de luceros apagados,
mis colinas translúcidas, manantiales del pecho
que dan el primer sustento de la especie.
Salientes del costillar, móvil cintura,
vasija colmada y tibia de mi vientre.

Amo la curva lunar de mis caderas
modeladas por alternas gestaciones,
la vasta redondez de ola de mis glúteos;
y mis piernas y pies, cimiento y sostén del templo.

Amo el puñado de pétalos oscuros, el oculto vellón
que guarda el misterioso umbral del paraíso,
la húmeda oquedad donde la sangre fluye
y brota el agua viva.

Este cuerpo mío doliente que se enferma,
que supura, que tose, que transpira,
secreta humores y heces y saliva,
y se fatiga, se agota, se marchita.

Cuerpo vivo, eslabón que asegura
la cadena infinita de cuerpos sucesivos.
Amo este cuerpo hecho con el lodo más puro:
semilla, raíz, savia, flor y fruto.

CELEBRATION OF THE BODY

I love this body that's lived through life,
its amphora shape, its water smoothness,
its streaming hair that crowns the skull,
the delicate stem of its crystal face
ascending exquisitely from shoulders and collarbones.

I love my back sprayed with muted bright stars,
my translucent hills, wellsprings of the breast
that provide primary sustenance to the species.
Cliff-like rib cage, waist in motion,
my womb a warm, overflowing vessel.

I love the moon-like curve of my hips
shaped by successive births,
the sharp curving wave of my ass;
and my legs and feet, foundation and support for the temple.

I love its handful of dark petals, its hidden fleece
that guards the mysterious entrance to paradise,
the damp cave from which blood flows
and birth-water springs.

This suffering body of mine that gets sick,
that leaks, that coughs, that sweats,
secretes humors and feces and spit,
gets tired, worn out, fades away.

Living body, a link that insures
an infinite chain of successive bodies.
I love this body made of the richest mud:
seeds, roots, sap, flowers and fruit.

NO-MAN'S-LAND

TIERRA DE NADIE

TIERRA DE NADIE

A mis poetas que quiero

Somos territorio minado en claridad,
quien traspasa el alambrado, resucita.
¿Pero a quién le interesa trepar en la espesura?
¿Quién se atreve a cruzar la tempestad?
¿Alguien quiere mirar de frente a la pureza?

Por eso nos han cercado en esta tierra de nadie,
bajo fuego cruzado y permanente.

NO-MAN'S-LAND

To the poets I love

We are a minefield of clarity,
and whoever crosses the barbed wire comes back to life.
But who's interested in crawling through undergrowth?
Who dares sail a tempest?
Who wants to come face to face with purity?

That's why we're fenced off in this no-man's-land,
under permanent crossfire.

CARTA A JOSÉ CORONEL URTECHO

Don José:

Le debía esta carta desde el primer encuentro.
Desde esa noche que usted seguramente no recuerda,
leyendo "A Luis Rosales lo esperamos en el Río San Juan."

De nuestros interminables
                    intermitentes paseos
suspensos de vez en cuando bajo la sombra amarilla
                    de una acacia,
con fondo de tractores y calles de tierra apelmazada,
polvorientas aceras y furgones de caña
                    recién cortada,
nunca le había hablado en otras cartas.

Quién hubiera previsto nuestro segundo encuentro
viéndonos cuando podíamos
                    en los atrios de iglesias,
                            las paradas de buses
                                    y los parques
en medio del exilio, la angustia,
                    la muerte y la esperanza.

Hasta ahora le vengo soltando estas palabras
como soltar una trenza oscura y apretada
y dejar el pelo solo, al aire suelto,
alzar su propio vuelo.

LETTER TO JOSÉ CORONEL URTECHO

Don José:

I've owed you this letter since the first time we met,
an evening you surely don't remember,
when you read "We Await Luis Rosales at San Juan River."

I've never talked about our endless
                    intermittent strolls
        (pausing now and then beneath the yellow shade
                    of an acacia,
        the background of tractors and packed dirt streets,
        dusty sidewalks, boxcars of fresh cut
                    sugar cane)
in my other letters.

Who could have foreseen our second encounter,
seeing each other when we could
                    in church atriums,
                        at bus stops,
                            in parks,
        in the middle of exile, anguish,
                    death and hope.

Only now am I releasing these words
as if untying a dark, tight braid
to let the loose hair fly
freely in the air.

Todo lo que hablábamos ya se volvió cierto,
y están vivas las palabras, y respiran,
y por primera vez podemos agarrarlas
como se agarra un güis, un pato aguja,
                una chorchita,
no para hacerles daño, sino para soltarlos
a volar en el más bello verano en La Azucena.

Las palabras han adquirido la forma concreta de las cosas,
y hasta su Río San Juan llegan hechas escuelas,
                talleres de artesanías,
centros de producción agrícola, desarrollos ganaderos.
Llegan vueltas bibliotecas,
                centros de salud,
                        cooperativas,
y en el antiguo puerto de San Carlos
la primera Casa de Cultura de su historia.

Usted piensa ahora que lo he olvidado
cuando todos los días he venido hablándole
esas bellas palabras que en nuestros viejos paseos
sólo eran sueños.

De todos modos, las pongo por escrito
para que conste en su historia y en la mía.
Como juntar un ramo de madroños y pascuas,
se las envío húmedas, olorosas y blancas.

Everything we talked about came true,
the words are alive, breathing,
and for the first time we can grab them
the way one might a great kiskadee, darter,
                    or yellow-tailed oriole—
not to hurt them, but set them free
to fly through a beautiful summer in La Azucena.

Those words have taken the concrete shape of things,
and as far away as your San Juan River they have turned into schools,
                    artisans' workshops,
agricultural production centers, and cattle developments.
They arrive as libraries,
                    health centers,
                                        cooperatives,
and in the ancient port of San Carlos
as the first Cultural Center in its history.

You think I've forgotten you
while every day I've been talking to you
in those beautiful words that in our old walks
were merely dreams.

Anyway, as proof of it I'm writing them down
so it's recorded in your history and mine.
Like gathering a bouquet of *madroño* and breath-of-heaven flowers,
I send them to you fresh, fragrant and pure.

(Lo imagino ahora de inevitable boina, bastón
        y blanca camisa manga larga,
leyendo o conversando o cerrando a las seis de la tarde
        las puertas de la casa;
o tal vez asomado al corredor hacia el Río Medio Queso
        esperando mi llegada
                o esta carta.)

(I imagine you now with your inevitable beret, cane
and long-sleeved white shirt,
reading or conversing or closing the doors to your house
against mosquitoes at six in the evening;
or maybe leaning from your porch looking out at Medio Queso River
waiting for my arrival
or for this letter.)

José Coronel Urtecho (1906-1994), Nicaraguan poet.

"We Await Luis Rosales at San Juan River" is the title of a Coronel Urtecho essay
about the Spanish poet Luis Rosales, and the reference is to his reading this essay
aloud to a very small group of people, among them Daisy Zamora, who, already
involved in the fledgling FSLN resistance to the Somoza regime, was working as a
teacher for workers' children at a sugar refinery. Eventually, she would be forced into
exile as a result of her activities in the Sandinista struggle, and would meet José
Coronel Urtecho again while both were in exile in Costa Rica before the Sandinistas
took power in 1979.

Madroño (*Calycophyllum candidissimum*) is the national tree of Nicaragua—one of
its common names in English is lemonwood.

La Azucena is where José Coronel Urtecho lived in the San Juan River area of
Nicaragua, and the Medio Queso River, which flowed by his house, is a tributary of
the San Juan.

ENCUENTRO SUBREPTICIO CON JOAQUÍN PASOS

Es difícil hablarte mientras me desgasto,
no es fácil platicar con vos, encontrarme con vos
en las gasolineras, en las antesalas de clínicas y oficinas,
en los embotellamientos de tráfico, Joaquinillo
                —¿puedo llamarte así?

Aquí hay mucho ruido. No me convence
el lino impecable de tus trajes,
ni tus poses de niño bien nacido.
           Sé
que sos pecador y católico, puro e impúdico.
Somos buenos para nada, inservibles para todo
             menos para el amor y el canto,
pero a nadie le importa el amor, nadie necesita del canto.

¿Qué hacemos, Joaquín, para dónde agarramos?
Tus carcajadas tampoco me convencen
y los lagartos se ríen de vos y de nosotros.
Ah, qué divertido, Joaquinillo, qué divertido
ver cómo te quebrás el alma.

¿Qué travesía inclemente nos espera?
Los pasajeros de tu barco estamos locos
porque un buque de letras navega solamente
en ingrávidos mares de agua de colonia.

Yo me iría a esos países tuyos de resplandecientes
           árboles de metal contra un sol nórdico,
entre los buenos muchachos alemanes hechos de queso,
vagaría en tu Luxemburgo de pequeñas mujeres
y nos revolcaríamos en alguna habitación de aquel hotel
           de comedor malva y oro,

SURREPTITIOUS ENCOUNTER WITH JOAQUÍN PASOS

It's difficult to speak with you when I'm worn out,
it's not so easy to chat, coming across you
in gas stations, the waiting rooms of clinics and offices,
and traffic jams, Joaquinillo
              —may I call you that?

It's so noisy here. Your impeccable linen
suits don't convince me, and I see through
that good-boy front you put up.
                I know
you're a sinner and a Catholic, pure and shameless.
We are good for nothing, useless for everything
            except love and poetry,
but nobody cares about love, and nobody needs poetry.

So what can we do, Joaquín, and where can we go?
Your outbursts of laughter don't convince me either,
your alligators laugh at us all.
Ah, how funny, Joaquinillo, how amusing
to watch the way you crush your soul.

What inclement voyage awaits us?
The passengers of your ship are all of us crazy
because a vessel made of words only sails
on weightless seas of eau de cologne.

I would travel to those countries of yours with shining
            metal trees reflecting Nordic sun,
among good German kids made of cheese,
I would roam your Luxembourg of small women
and we'd go wild and roll around a room in that hotel
           with a mauve and gold dining room,

y desde la ventana le arrojaríamos monedas
al flautista polaco
o contemplaríamos la orquesta de zíngaros suicidas.

¿Por qué llorás por un pescado muerto?
¿Por qué te conmovés ante el cadáver de una pájara?

Mejor te dejo. Aquí hay mucho ruido
y sólo el ajetreo importa, aunque nadie sepa por qué,
ni para dónde vamos.
Es justo que te deje reposar al abrigo de tus pecados
mortales y capitales.
Me has dicho que te vas a morir de angustia una madrugada.
Ya vas a ver cómo, cuando llegués a tu correspondiente
naufragio, hay suspiros de alivio.
Al fin la familia descansa de la oveja negra o blanca.

Estoy ensordecida, sin tiempo para encontrar . . .
Los cementerios y parques están abandonados,
una multitud de niños muertos nos miran con sus ojos ciegos.
Dame alguna señal, Joaquín, alguna señal
en estas latitudes
lejanas.

and throw coins from the window
　　　　to the Polish flute player
or contemplate the orchestra of suicidal gypsies.

Why do you weep for a dead fish?
Why are you moved by the carcass of a bird?

It's better that I leave you. It's so noisy here
and only rushing around matters, though no one knows why,
　　　　　　　　　　or where we're all going.
It's fair to let you rest, sheltered by your mortal
　　　　　　　　　　and deadly sins.
You've told me you'll die of anguish some dawn.
Just wait and see, when you reach your respective
　　　　shipwreck, there will be sighs of relief.
At last, the family will get a rest from the black or white sheep.

I'm deafened, with no time to search for . . .
The graveyards and parks are deserted,
crowds of dead children stare at us with blind eyes.
Give me a signal, Joaquín, any signal
in these isolated
　　　　zones.

Joaquín Pasos (1914-1947), Nicaraguan poet (also referred to here as
"Joaquinillo," a Spanish diminutive for Joaquín). One of the founding members
of the Nicaraguan *Vanguardia* movement, Pasos was a brilliant writer who died
in his early thirties of tuberculosis, leaving behind a highly original body of work
that has had a powerful influence on contemporary Nicaraguan literature. Daisy
Zamora's poem alludes to lines throughout his poetry, but readers can easily enjoy
her poem without knowing exact references, too numerous to annotate. As
implied in the poem, Pasos' work can be quite imaginative. For example, his only
verifiable trip beyond the borders of Nicaragua was to visit a doctor in
neighboring Costa Rica near the end of his life; nonetheless, he wrote a series of
international travel poems, aptly titled *Poems of a Young Man Who Never Traveled.*
In that same spirit, he wrote a series of love poems titled *Poems of a Young Man
Who Never Loved,* and a fascinating series of poems written in English (he was
self-taught) called *Poems of a Young Man Who Knows No English.*

ARS AMANDI

A: *Ernesto Cardenal*

Yo nací también para un amor extremista.
Y conozco a tantos y tantas que buscan ese amor
y no lo encuentran. Y cuántas y cuántos
que sin saberlo siquiera, lo poseen.

Yo, que no soy deidad, ni mucho menos,
pero que soy mujer
entrenada en el amor desde en los tiempos de la Diosa,
puedo asegurarlo: quienes amamos
vivimos en universos paralelos.

Sin conocer a Dios, sé lo que es dar vida
                              dando ya la muerte.
Que salga desde dentro de mí una criatura
            diferente a mí, pero que es mi reflejo—
                  independiente de mí, pero perteneciéndome.

El amor espiritual
no es sentimental ni mercenario.
Me atrevo a decir que el amor por la criatura propia
también puede ser perfecto:
                  ni aridez ni ausencias lo doblegan.

Amar a Dios como opuesto
porque lo opuesto se junta: Simbiosis mística.
El celibato es matrimonio.
Los que amamos somos eternamente célibes.

THE ART OF LOVING

For Ernesto Cardenal

I too was born for extremist love,
and know so many who search for that love
but never find it, and even more
who possess it without knowing.

No deity, far less than that,
but simply a woman
trained in love since the time of the Goddess,
I can assure you: those of us who love
exist in parallel worlds.

Even without knowing God, I know what it means to give life
                              which also means giving death.
Because a child may come from inside me
            different from me, but my reflection—
            independent of me, but my possession.

Spiritual love
isn't sentimental or mercenary.
I dare say love for one's own child
can also be perfect:
            no aridity, no absences can crush it.

To love god as an opposite
because opposites attract: Mystical symbiosis.
Celibacy, then, is marriage.
We who truly love can also be eternal celibates.

La dulzura del enamoramiento es pasajera.
Una tarde en París, a la luz del otoño,
parejas apasionadas en cines, parques, plazas,
me hicieron llorar. Y son incontables las veces
que las caricias de otros me conmueven.

Está fuera del juego erótico . . . y no me río.
Probó ya nada menos que el placer Divino,
tan intenso como un dolor insoportable,
tan definitivo como morir en vida.
Dios y su alma fundidos en la caricia sin tacto:
la perfección del erotismo puro.

Pero la historia de un amor verdadero
es siempre una historia de amor y soledad.
De honda soledad, de soledad sola, así, parada en seco.

La suerte de ser correspondido.
Sor Juana, por ejemplo, también amó en extremo
y Dios no le dió entrada. El cielo se cerró hostil
al ambicioso vuelo de su espíritu.
La noche de Sor Juana fue en verdad oscura,
noche inmensa, construída a pulso sobre el vacío.[1]

Experto en erotismo sin los sentidos,
debe entender la angustia del poeta Bandeira
por su alma, que le arruinaba el amor
al no encontrar satisfacción
en otra alma.
Las almas —decía, *son incomunicables.*
Y también dijo: . . . *al contacto de mis manos lentas,*
la sustancia de tu carne
es igual a la del silencio.[2]

The sweetness of falling in love is fleeting.
One evening in Paris, in autumn light,
passionate couples in cinemas, parks and plazas
made me cry. And countless times
the affection of others has moved me.

You're out of the erotic game . . . and I don't laugh.
You've experienced nothing less than divine pleasure
as intense as unbearable pain,
as definitive as dying while staying alive.
God and your soul melted into a caress without touch:
the perfection of absolute eroticism.

But the history of a true love
is always one of love and solitude.
Of deep solitude, supreme solitude, up against it.

Not everyone has the luck of requited love.
Sor Juana, for example, also loved in the extreme,
but God shut her out. A hostile heaven shut
to the ambitious flight of her spirit.
Her night was truly dark,
immense night, built inch by inch over emptiness.[1]

As an expert in eroticism without the senses,
surely you understand the anguish of the poet Bandeira
for his soul, which ruined love
finding no satisfaction
in other souls.
Souls, he said, *cannot communicate.*
He also said: . . . *to the touch of my slow hands*
                the substance of your flesh
                is that of silence.[2]

Si de no esperar nada se trata el amor místico,
puedo entenderlo:
La sustancia del amor está hecha de silencios,
de plenitud de ausencia.

Sin vislumbrar el Rostro de la Belleza,
amo lo bello efímero,
pero también amo lo que no es:

... que unos párpados cerrados
recuerden un poema de Eluard
y que se acaricie en unos brazos
alguna cosa más allá de la carne, que se los toque
como al ámbar de una tarde.[3]

Lo erótico va más allá del cuerpo.
El que amo ha de morir, y yo moriré también.
En el gozo del más íntimo abrazo
tiemblan estremecidos nuestros cuerpos
que morirán, no importa cuánto nos amemos.

Pero mi amor no se engorda ni aburguesa,
y el rostro del amado, para mí, no envejece.

Amar aceptando que no poseo al otro,
y que yo me pertenezco sólo a mí misma.
Nuestros cuerpos se unen
respondiendo al deseo con el deseo,
pero nunca serán un sólo cuerpo.

Amar sin miedo a la soledad
y al tiempo.

If mystical love is about expecting nothing,
I can understand it:
Love's substance is made of silences
and complete absence.

Without a clue about "Absolute Beauty,"
I love ephemeral beauty,
but also love the unseen:

. . . that some closed eyelids
bring to mind a poem of Eluard's,
and arms one might caress
are more than flesh, one touches them
as if they are the amber of afternoon.[3]

The erotic goes beyond the body.
The one I love will die, and I will too.
In the joy of the most intimate embrace
our bodies that tremble and shiver
will die no matter how deeply we love.

But my love doesn't grow fat or bourgeois,
and the face of the beloved, for me, doesn't age.

To love accepting that I don't possess the other,
and that I belong only to myself.
Our bodies unite,
answering desire with desire,
but they will never become one body.

To love without fear of loneliness
or time.

Los convencionalismos son enemigos del amor.
Vivir en el amor es asumir los riesgos.

Inauguraron el nuevo mausoleo
donde reposará Su Eminencia.
Asistió: "... toda la clase política,
que se dieron la paz y se abrazaron."

(Una secuencia de Fellini.)

Afuera, bajo el crisol del sol, la multitud espera:
Las tres cuartas partes de los grandes momentos históricos
se han pasado, en todas partes, esperando.[4]

Jerarcas y políticos son enemigos del amor.
Han idealizado el poder de la espada,
pero hablan en nombre de Dios y del amor,
                                    y viven de eso.

La transformación del sistema, ni usted ni yo la veremos.
La multitud, en todas partes, sigue esperando.

Mujeres de los políticos, me dan lástima.
(¿Creerán en ellos?)

Compañeras clandestinas de curas y jerarcas,
me dan más lástima.

Entiendo su renuncia por amor a Dios
porque es amor verdadero.
(Usted no esconde a ninguna pobre mujer bajo su cama).
Renuncia y entrega también es amor.
(Por eso nunca entendí el poder).

Conventionalities are enemies of love.
To live in love is to assume the risks.

The new mausoleum where "His
Eminence" will rest was inaugurated.
Present: ". . . the whole political world,
all embracing and wishing peace to one another."

(A Fellini sequence.)

Outside, beneath the crucible of the sun, the multitude waits:
*For three-quarters of the great historical moments
everywhere they have been left waiting.*[4]

Church leaders and politicians are enemies of love.
They've idealized the power of the sword,
but speak in the name of God and love,
                                    and live off it.

Neither you nor I will see the transformation of the system.
Multitudes, everywhere, still waiting.

Wives of politicians, I feel sorry for them.
(Could they possibly trust them?)

Secret lovers of priests and church leaders
I pity even more.

I understand your renunciation for the love of God
because it's true love.
(You don't hide any poor women under your bed.)
Renunciation and dedication is also love.
(That's why I never understood power).

Conozco a extremistas del amor
que ni siquiera tienen el consuelo divino,
ni el poder,
sólo el poder de su amor extremo.

No todos los versos de amor se escriben en vano.[5]

[1] Sor Juana Inés de la Cruz (1651-1695). Intelectual, poeta y dramaturga Mexicana. Monja Carmelita de la Orden de San Jerónimo.
[2] Manuel Bandeira (1886-1968). Poeta Brasileño. La primera cita se refiere a un verso del poema "Arte de Amar", *Belo Belo* (1948); la segunda es del poema "O Siléncio", *O Ritmo Dissoluto* (1924).
[3] Vinícius de Moraes (b. 1913). Poeta Brasileño. Versos seleccionados del poema "Receita de Mulher."
[4] Marguerite Yourcenar, *Le Labyrinthe du monde III: Quoi? L'Etérnité* (1988).
[5] Se refiere a un poema del libro *Epigramas*, del poeta Nicaragüense Ernesto Cardenal:

> Muchachas que algún día leáis emocionadas estos versos
> y soñéis con un poeta:
> sabed que yo los hice para una como vosotras
> y que fué en vano.

I know extremists of love
who have no divine consolation,
and no power
but that of their extreme love.

So not all poems of love are written in vain.[5]

[1] Sor Juana Inés de la Cruz (1651-1695). Mexican poet, playwright, and scholar. A Carmelite nun in the Order of Saint Jerome.

[2] Manuel Bandeira (1886-1968). Brazilian poet. The first quotation is a line from his poem "Arte de Amar" ("The Art of Loving"), *Belo Belo* (1948); the second is from the poem "O Siléncio" ("The Silence"), *O Ritmo Dissoluto* (1924).

[3] Vinícius de Moraes (b. 1913). Brazilian poet. Excerpted from the poem "Receita de Mulher" ("Recipe of a Woman").

[4] Marguerite Yourcenar, *Le Labyrinthe du monde III: Quoi? L'Etérnité* [*What? Eternity*] (1988).

[5] Reference is to a poem from Nicaraguan poet Ernesto Cardenal's book *Epigramas* (*Epigrams*):

> Girls who some day read and are moved by these verses
> and dream of a poet:
> know that I made them for one like you
> but that it was in vain.

DAISY ZAMORA won Nicaragua's National Poetry Prize, *Mariano Fiallos Gil*, in 1977. Author of three widely read books of poetry in Spanish, and the editor of a popular anthology of Nicaraguan women poets, she also edited a book about the concepts of cultural politics during the Sandinista Revolution. A combatant in the National Sandinista Liberation Front (FSLN), and program director for the clandestine Radio Sandino, she became Vice-Minister of Culture after the triumph of the revolution. Her poems, essays, articles and translations have been published in magazines and literary newspapers throughout Latin America, the Caribbean, the U.S., Canada, Europe and Australia. Her poems appear in more than forty anthologies in Spanish, English, German, Swedish, Italian, Bulgarian, Russian, Vietnamese, Chinese, Dutch, Flemish, Slovak and Czech. Other English translations of her work include *Clean Slate* (Curbstone, 1993), *Riverbed of Memory* (City Lights) and *Life for Each* (Katabasis Press, England). She has given poetry readings and lectures throughout the world, including many venues in the U.S., and was a featured artist in Bill Moyers' PBS series about poetry, *The Language of Life*.

GEORGE EVANS is the author of five books of poetry, including *The New World* (Curbstone Press, 2002). He has been a recipient of writing fellowships from the National Endowment for the Arts, the California Arts Council, the Lannan Foundation, and a *Monbusho* fellowship from the Japanese government for the study of Japanese poetry. Founder and editor of the popular public arts project *Streetfare Journal*, displaying contemporary poetry and photography on buses in U.S. cities, he is also the editor of *Charles Olson & Cid Corman: Complete Correspondence* (National Poetry Foundation: University of Maine, Orono), and has translated extensively from the work of Vietnamese poet Huu Thinh.

CURBSTONE PRESS, INC.

is a non-profit publishing house dedicated to literature that reflects a commitment to social change, with an emphasis on contemporary writing from Latino, Latin American and Vietnamese cultures. Curbstone presents writers who give voice to the unheard in a language that goes beyond denunciation to celebrate, honor and teach. Curbstone builds bridges between its writers and the public – from inner-city to rural areas, colleges to community centers, children to adults. Curbstone seeks out the highest aesthetic expression of the dedication to human rights and intercultural understanding: poetry, testimonies, novels, stories, and children's books.

This mission requires more than just producing books. It requires ensuring that as many people as possible learn about these books and read them. To achieve this, a large portion of Curbstone's schedule is dedicated to arranging tours and programs for its authors, working with public school and university teachers to enrich curricula, reaching out to underserved audiences by donating books and conducting readings and community programs, and promoting discussion in the media. It is only through these combined efforts that literature can truly make a difference.

Curbstone Press, like all non-profit presses, depends on the support of individuals, foundations, and government agencies to bring you, the reader, works of literary merit and social significance which might not find a place in profit-driven publishing channels, and to bring the authors and their books into communities across the country. Our sincere thanks to the many individuals, foundations, and government agencies who support this endeavor: J. Walton Bissell Foundation, Connecticut Commission on the Arts, Connecticut Humanities Council, Daphne Seybolt Culpeper Foundation, Fisher Foundation, Greater Hartford Arts Council, Hartford Courant Foundation, J. M. Kaplan Fund, Eric Mathieu King Fund, Lannan Foundation, John D. and Catherine T. MacArthur Foundation, National Endowment for the Arts, Open Society Institute, Puffin Foundation, and the Woodrow Wilson National Fellowship Foundation.

Please help to support Curbstone's efforts to present the diverse voices and views that make our culture richer. Tax-deductible donations can be made by check or credit card to:
Curbstone Press, 321 Jackson Street, Willimantic, CT 06226
phone: (860) 423-5110   fax: (860) 423-9242
www.curbstone.org

IF YOU WOULD LIKE TO BE A MAJOR SPONSOR OF A
PARTICULAR BOOK, PLEASE CONTACT US.